The Authoritarian Attempt
To Capture Education

The Authoritarian Attempt
To Capture Education

PAPERS FROM THE 2D CONFERENCE ON

The Scientific Spirit & Democratic Faith

Vol. 2

Essay Index Reprint Series

BOOKS FOR LIBRARIES PRESS
FREEPORT, NEW YORK

INTERNATIONAL STANDARD BOOK NUMBER:

0-8369-1819-3

LIBRARY OF CONGRESS CATALOG CARD NUMBER:

76-121458

PRINTED IN THE UNITED STATES OF AMERICA

PREFACE

A BOVE THE DRONE of the fighter planes, the shriek of the bombs, and the roar of the heavy shells, the hoarse voice of reaction rises over the earth. The war itself is only symptomatic; it is evidence of the world's sickness, not the sickness itself. When the war is finally ended, the basic struggle will nevertheless still go on. We talk about this struggle in hackneyed phrases, because it is not easy to say just what we mean by it. We say that it is the struggle between those who would dominate and exploit human beings for their own ends, and those who would free them for the realization in common of their best possibilities. Or we say that it is a struggle for power between a privileged minority, with wealth increasingly concentrated in fewer hands, and the great masses of mankind.

Complicated as is the power struggle, however, the problem carries us deeper beneath the surface than this, and is more complicated. For underlying that struggle is the challenge to intelligence. Is there mind enough in the world to realize some of the possibilities for freer and more democratic living inherent in scientific progress? In an age of high-octane gasoline and radar, what comparable knowledge will enable us to exploit our resources to the common advantage? Is the method of science applicable to gadgets alone, or can it help us to pick our way through the complexities of the present and the uncertainties of the future? And if we do get to see the path we ought to follow, shall we be free to follow it?

When the second Conference on the Scientific Spirit and Democratic Faith convened at the Meeting House of the New York Society for Ethical Culture, the atmosphere was pregnant with such questions as these. The Conference is a coming together of scientists, philosophers, educators, religious leaders, and others in their common concern for the future of the free mind and the free spirit. They are dedicated to keeping the ways open for free inquiry, believing that free inquiry and democracy are as inseparable as print and the page upon which it appears.

There are those who insist that democracy and the very idea of the brotherhood of man are dependent on belief in the fatherhood of God. The participants in this Conference believe, rather, that there are many ways of feeling the push and pull of the universe, in William James's phrase, and that none of them has been shown to be essential to the democratic way of life. They are not dogmatic in their insistence on any one truth or any set of truths. They believe that all truths, whatever their origin, are established by the scientific method. They hold no part of human experience sacrosanct, nor any domain of belief a special preserve to be guarded from the scrutiny of the scientist. Hence the Conference on the Scientific Spirit and Democratic Faith has nothing in common with those who insist that they are in possession of *the* way and *the* truth, and that the method of authority is the best way of fixing belief.

The reaction which exploits the basic struggle of our time uses the method of authority as one of its indispensable techniques. Fascism is not its only name or form, but it is the one of which we have been made most conscious during the past two decades. Looking backward, we know now that fascism was bred in misery and struggle: the misery of millions on breadlines and in hovels, and the struggle for power in which group was pitted against group. It fed on men's fears and anxieties; it grew by brutality, mysticism, and an adept usage of lies and racist nonsense; and by using the ancient principle of "divide and conquer," it shrewdly elbowed its way through potentially stronger forces, to gain dominance both at home and abroad.

It was in this world of snowballing brute power that the American people listened to arguments in behalf of individualism, isolationism, and the sanctity of detached and "pure" research. The *laissez-faire* liberal tradition enjoined us to stand on our own feet and become the best men and women we could—as if standing shoulder to shoulder with others made one less himself! The nationalist tradition commanded us to be ever wary and suspicious of "foreigners" and to provide for our own national security— as if joining with the other peace forces of the world could make us less secure! The scientific tradition was interpreted as making the pursuit of truth conditional upon a monastic, cloistered life—as if a scientist were any less dedicated or less objective if he become conscious of his responsibilities to the society in which he lives! All this was like manna from heaven to the fascist users of "divide and conquer" tactics. For extreme individualism, isolationism, and social irresponsibility—however unconscious or unintentional—are the procurers of fascism.

We wish that all this were as a story that is told, or a nightmare that is ended. But the day may soon come when fascism, too, is but an evil shadow falling across the pages of history, while reaction seeks other names and other forms to gain or keep ascendancy. It was with this knowledge of the long-range problems ahead of us and a deep conviction that in the fight against reaction the scientific spirit and democratic faith are inseparable allies, that the Conference was formed.

Its purposes may be said to be threefold. First, to resist the method of authority and the forces of authoritarianism in whatever guise they show themselves. Second, to bridge the gaps separating specialists in different fields of inquiry and interest, in the attempt to get further clarification of their common problems. Third, and most important of all, to make what specific contributions it can in the struggle against reaction and in forwarding the development of democracy by having its views carry over into our common life—not through any "direct action," but by pointing ways in which scientific method can and ought to play an integral part in the shaping of democratic policy. These are, to be sure, far-reaching aims, and the participants in the Conference are altogether conscious of the modesty of their achievement. It is because they are convinced of the necessity of the task that they are committed to the performance of it.

The papers that follow are now published, with some abridgements, as they were presented at the 1944 Conference. It was in the belief that certain organized movements in education constituted a threat to the scientific spirit and democratic faith that its attention was concentrated on the educational issue. The pages of this volume are a documentation of that belief, and of the relation of this issue to the larger fight against reaction. Although the Conference has made positive inroads in this area, the struggle over democratic education continues and will continue. In the nature of things, there can be no guarantees about the outcome of it, or of the larger and even more fateful struggle. There is a certain security, however, in the knowledge that such men are joined in the common cause. Our generation is called upon to make great decisions. If we can pave the way for the education of free men, we may help to build a free world.

JEROME NATHANSON

New York City
March 8, 1945

TABLE OF CONTENTS

1

THE DEMOCRATIC FAITH
AND EDUCATION

John Dewey

NOT EVEN THE MOST FAR-SEEING of men could have predicted, no longer ago than fifty years, the course events have taken. The expectations that were entertained by men of generous outlook are in fact chiefly notable in that the actual course of events has moved, and with violence, in the opposite direction. The ardent and hopeful social idealist of the last century or so has been proved so wrong that a reaction to the opposite extreme has taken place. A recent writer has even proposed a confraternity of pessimists who should live together in some sort of social oasis. It is a fairly easy matter to list the articles of that old faith which, from the standpoint of today, have been tragically frustrated.

The first article on the list had to do with the prospects of the abolition of war. It was held that the revolution which was taking place in commerce and communication would break down the barriers which had kept the peoples of the earth alien and hostile and would create a state of interdependence which in time would ensure lasting peace. Only an extreme pessimist ventured to suggest that interdependence might multiply points of friction and conflict. Another item of that creed was the belief that a general development of enlightenment and rationality was bound to follow the increase in knowledge, and its diffusion, that would result from the revolution in science which was taking place. Since it had long been held that rationality and freedom were intimately allied, it was held that the movement toward democratic institutions and popular government which had produced in succession the British, American, and French Revolutions was bound to spread until freedom and equality were the foundations of political government in every country of the globe.

A time of general ignorance and popular unenlightenment and a time of despotic and oppressive governmental rule were taken to be practically synonymous. Hence the third article of faith. There was a general belief among social philosophers that governmental activities were necessarily more or less oppressive; that governmental action tended to be an artificial interference with the operation of natural laws. Consequently the spread of enlightenment and democratic institutions would produce a gradual but assured withering away of the powers of the political state. Freedom was supposed to be so deeply rooted in the very nature of man that given the spread of rational enlightenment it would take care of itself with only a minimum of political action confined to ensuring external police order.

The other article of faith to be mentioned was the general belief that the vast, the almost incalculable, increase in productivity resulting from the industrial revolution was bound to raise the general standard of living to a point where extreme poverty would be practically eliminated. It was believed that the opportunity to lead a decent, self-respecting, because self-sufficient, economic life would be assured to every one who was physically and morally normal.

The course of events culminating in the present situation suffices to show without any elaborate argument how grievously these generous expectations have been disappointed. Instead of universal peace, there are two wars, worldwide in extent and destructive beyond anything known in all history. Instead of uniform and steady growth of democratic freedom and equality, we have the rise of powerful totalitarian states with thorough-going suppression of liberty of belief and expression, outdoing the most despotic states of previous history. We have an actual growth in importance and range of governmental action in legislation and administration as necessary means of rendering freedom on the part of the many an assured actual fact. Instead of promotion of economic security and movement toward the elimination of poverty, we have had a great increase in the extent and the intensity of industrial crises with great increase of inability of workers to find employment. Social instability has reached a point that may portend revolution if it goes on unchecked.

Externally it looks as if the pessimists had the best of the case. But before we reach a conclusion on that point, we have to inquire concerning the solidity of the premise upon which the idealistic optimists rested their case. This principle was that the desirable goals held in view were to be accomplished by a complex of forces to which in their entirety the name "Nature" was given. In practical effect, acceptance of this principle was equivalent to adoption of a policy of drift as far as human intelligence and effort were concerned. No conclusion is warranted until we have inquired how far failure and frustration are consequences of putting our trust in a policy of drift; a policy of letting "George" in the shape of Nature and Natural Law do the work which only human intelligence and effort could possibly accomplish. No conclusion can be reached until we have considered an alternative: What is likely to happen if we recognize that the responsibility for creating a state of peace internationally, and of freedom and economic security internally, has to be carried by deliberate cooperative human effort? Technically speaking, the policy known as *laissez-faire* is one of limited application. But its limited and technical significance is one instance of a manifestation of wide-spread trust in the ability of impersonal forces, popularly called Nature, to do a work that has in fact to be done by human insight, foresight, and purposeful planning.

Not all the men of the earlier period were of the idealistic type. The idealistic philosophy was a positive factor in permitting those who prided themselves upon being realistic to turn events so as to produce consequences dictated by their own private and class advantage. The failure of cooperative and collective intelligence and effort to intervene was an invitation to immediate short term intervention by those who had an eye to their own profit. The consequences were wholesale destruction and waste of natural resources, increase of social instability, and mortgaging of the future to a transitory and brief present of so-called prosperity. If "idealists" were misguided in what they failed to do, "realists" were wrong in what they did. If the former erred in supposing that the drift (called by them progress or evolution) was inevitably toward the better, the latter were more actively harmful because their insistence upon trusting to natural laws was definitely in the interest of personal and class profit.

The omitted premise in the case of both groups is the fact that neither science nor technology is an impersonal cosmic force. They operate only in the medium of human desire, foresight, aim, and effort. Science and technology are transactions in which man and nature work together and in which the human factor is that directly open to modification and direction. That man takes part along with physical conditions in invention and use of the devices, implements, and machinery of industry and commerce no one would think of denying.

But in practice, if not in so many words, it has been denied that man has any responsibility for the consequences that result from what he invents and employs. This denial is implicit in our widespread refusal to engage in large-scale collective planning. Not a day passes, even in the present crisis, when the whole idea of such planning is not ridiculed as an emanation from the brain of starry-eyed professors or of others equally inept in practical affairs. And all of this in the face of the fact that there is not a successful industrial organization that does not owe its success to persistent planning within a limited field—with an eye to profit—to say nothing of the terribly high price we have paid in the way of insecurity and war for putting our trust in drift.

Refusal to accept responsibility for looking ahead and for planning in matters national and international is based upon refusal to employ in social affairs, in the field of human relations, the methods of observation, interpretation, and test that are matters of course in dealing with physical things, and to which we owe the conquest of physical nature. The net result is a state of imbalance, of profoundly disturbed equilibrium between our physical knowledge and our social-moral knowledge. This lack of harmony is a powerful factor in producing the present crisis with all its tragic features. For physical knowledge and physical technology have far outstripped social or humane knowledge and human engineering. Our failure to use in matters of direct human concern the scientific methods which have revolutionized physical knowledge has permitted the latter to dominate the social scene.

The change in the physical aspect of the world has gone on so rapidly that there is probably no ground for surprise in the fact that our psychological and moral knowledge has not kept pace. But there is cause for astonishment in the fact that after the catastrophe of war, insecurity, and the threat to democratic institutions have shown the need for new moral and intellectual attitudes and habits that will correspond with the changed state of the world, there should be a definite campaign to make the scientific attitude the scapegoat for present evils, while a return to the beliefs and practices of a pre-scientific and pre-technological age is urged as the road to our salvation.

THE ORGANIZED ATTACK now being made against science and against technology as inherently materialistic and as usurping the place properly held by the abstract moral precepts—abstract because divorcing ends from the means by which they must be realized—defines the issue we now have to face. Shall we go backwards or shall we go ahead to discover and put into practice the means by which science and technology shall be made fundamental in the promotion of human welfare? The failure to use scientific methods in creating understanding of human relationships and interests and in planning measures and policies that correspond in human affairs to the technologies in physical use is easily explained in historical terms. The new science began with things at the furthest remove from human affairs, namely with the stars of the heavens. From astronomy the new methods went on to win their victories in physics and chemistry. Still later science was applied in physiological and biological subject-matter. At every stage, the advance met determined resistance from the representatives of established institutions who felt their prestige was bound up with maintenance of old beliefs and found their class-control of others being threatened. In consequence, many workers in science found that the easiest way in which to procure an opportunity to carry on their inquiries was to adopt an attitude of extreme specialization. The effect was equivalent to the position that their methods and conclusions were not and could not be "dangerous," since they had no point of contact with man's serious moral concerns. This position in turn served to perpetuate and confirm the older separation of man as man from the rest of nature and to intensify the split between the "material" and the moral and "ideal."

Thus it has come about that when scientific inquiry began to move from its virtually complete victories in astronomy and physics and its partial victory in the field of living things over into the field of human affairs and concerns, the interests and institutions that offered resistance to its earlier advance are now gathering themselves together for a final attack upon that aspect of science which in truth constitutes its supreme and culminating significance. On the principle that offense is the best defense, respect for science and loyalty to its outlook are attacked as the chief source of all our present social ills. One may read, for example, in current literature such a condescending concession as marks the following passage: "Of course, the scientific attitude, though often leading to such a catastrophe, is not to be condemned," the immediate context showing that the particular "catastrophe" in mind consists of "errors leading to war . . . derived from an incorrect theory of truth." Since these errors are produced by belief in the applicability of scientific method to human as well as physical facts, the remedy, according to this writer, is to abandon "the erroneous application of the methods and results of natural science to the problems of human life."

In three respects the passage is typical of the organized campaign now in active operation. There is first the assertion that such catastrophes as that of the present war are the result of devotion to scientific method and conclusions. The denunciation of "natural" science as applied to human affairs carries, in the second place, the implication that man is outside of and above nature, and the consequent necessity of returning to the medieval pre-scientific doctrine of a supernatural foundation and outlook in all social and moral subjects. Then, thirdly, there is the assumption, directly contrary to fact, that the scientific method has at the present time been seriously and systematically applied to the problems of human life.

I dignify the passage quoted by this reference to it because it serves quite as well as a multitude of other passages from reactionaries to convey a sense of the present issue. It is true that the results of natural science have had a large share, for evil as well as for good, in bringing the world to its present pass. But it is equally true that "natural" science has been identified with physical science in a sense in which the physical is set over against the human. It is true that the interests and institutions which are now attacking science are just the forces which, in behalf of a supernatural center of gravity, strive to maintain this tragic split in human affairs. Now the issue, as is becoming clearer every day, is whether we shall go backward or whether we shall go forward toward recognition in theory and practice of the indissoluble unity of the humanistic and the naturalistic.

WHAT HAS ALL THIS to do with education? The answer to this question may be gathered from the fact that those who are engaged in assault upon science center their attacks upon the increased attention given by our schools to science and to its application in vocational training. In a world which is largely what it is today because of science and technology they propose that education should turn its back upon even the degree of recognition science and technology have received. They propose we turn our face to the medievalism in which so-called "liberal" arts were identified with literary arts; a course natural to adopt in an age innocent of knowledge of nature, an age in which the literary arts were the readiest means of rising above barbarism through acquaintance with the achievements of Greek-Roman culture. Their proposal is so remote from the facts of the present world, it involves such a bland ignoring of actualities, that there is a temptation to dismiss it as idle vaporing. But it would be a tragic mistake to take the reactionary assaults so lightly. For they are an expression of just the forces that keep science penned up in a compartment labelled "materialistic and anti-human." They strengthen all the habits and institutions which render that which is morally "ideal" important in action and which leave the "material" to operate without humane direction.

Let me return for the moment to my initial statement that the basic error of social idealists was the assumption that something called "natural law" could be trusted, with only incidental cooperation by human beings, to bring about the desired ends. The lesson to be learned is that human attitudes and efforts are the strategic center for promotion of the general aims of peace among nations; promotion of economic security; the use of political means in order to advance freedom and equality, and the worldwide cause of democratic institutions. Anyone who starts from this premise is bound to see that it carries with it the basic importance of education in creating the habits and the outlook that are able and eager to secure the ends of peace, democracy, and economic stability.

When this is seen, it will also be seen how little has actually been done in our schools to render science and technology active agencies in creating the attitudes and dispositions and in securing the kinds of knowledge that are capable of coping with the problems of men and women today. Externally a great modification has taken place in subjects taught and in methods of teaching them. But when the changes are critically examined, it is found that they consist largely in emergency concessions and accommodation to the urgent conditions and issues of the contemporary world. The standards and the controlling methods in education are still mainly those of a pre-scientific and pre-technological age. This statement will seem to many persons to be exaggerated. But consider the purposes which still govern as a rule instruction in just those subjects that are taken to be decisively "modern," namely, science and vocational preparation. Science is taught upon the whole as a body of readymade information and technical skills. It is not taught as furnishing in its method the pattern for all effective intelligent conduct. It is taught upon the whole not with respect to the way in which it actually enters into human life, and hence as a supremely humanistic subject, but as if it had to do with a world which is "external" to human concerns. It is not presented in connection with the ways in which it actually enters into every aspect and phase of present human life. And it is hardly necessary to add that still less is it taught in connection with what scientific knowledge of human affairs might do in overcoming sheer drift. Scientific method and conclusions will not have gained a fundamentally important place in education until they are seen and treated as supreme agencies in giving direction to collective and cooperative human behavior.

The same sort of thing is to be said about the kind of use now made in education of practical and vocational subjects, so called. The reactionary critics are busy urging that the latter subjects be taught to the masses—who are said to be incapable of rising to the plane of the "intellectual" but who do the useful work which somebody has to do, and who may be taught by vocational education to do it more effectively. This view is, of course, an open and avowed attempt to return to that dualistic separation of ideas and action, of the "intellectual" and the "practical," of the liberal and servile arts, that marked the feudal age. And this reactionary move in perpetuation of the split from which the world is suffering is offered as a cure, a panacea, not as the social and moral quackery it actually is. As is the case with science, the thing supremely needful is to go forward. And the forward movement in the case of technology as in the case of science is to do away with the chasm which ancient and medieval educational practice and theory set up between the liberal and the vocational, not to treat the void, the hole, constituted by this chasm, as if it were a foundation for creation of a free society.

There is nothing whatever inherent in the occupations that are socially necessary and useful to divide them into those which are "learned" professions and the callings which are menial, servile, and illiberal. As far as such a separation exists in fact, it is an inheritance from the earlier class structure of human relations. It is a denial of democracy. At the very time when an important, perhaps *the* important, problem in education is to fill education having an occupational direction with a genuinely liberal content, we have, believe it or not, a movement, such as is sponsored, for example, by President Hutchins, to cut vocational training off from any contact with what is liberating by relegating it to special schools devoted to inculcation of technical skills. Inspiring vocational education with a liberal spirit and filling it with a liberal content is not a utopian dream. It is a demonstrated possibility in schools here and there in which subjects usually labelled "practically useful" are taught, charged with scientific understanding and with a sense of the universal social-moral applications they potentially possess.

IF LITTLE IS SAID in the foregoing remarks specifically upon the topic of democratic faith, it is because their bearing upon a democratic outlook largely appears upon their very face. Conditions in this country when the democratic philosophy of life and democratic institutions were taking shape were such as to encourage a belief that the latter were so natural to man, so appropriate to his very being, that if they were once established they would tend to maintain themselves. I cannot rehearse here the list of events that have given this naïve faith a shock. They are contained in every deliberate attack upon democracy and in every expression of cynicism about its past failures and pessimism about its future—attacks and expressions which have to be taken seriously if they are looked at as signs of trying to establish democracy as an end in separation from the concrete means upon which the end depends.

Democracy is not an easy road to take and follow. On the contrary, as far as its realization is concerned in the complex conditions of the contemporary world it is a supremely difficult one. Upon the whole we are entitled to take courage from the fact that it has worked as well as it has done. But to this courage we must add, if our courage is to be intelligent rather than blind, the fact that successful maintenance of democracy demands the utmost in use of the best available methods to procure a social knowledge that is reasonably commensurate with our physical knowledge, together with invention and use of forms of social engineering reasonably commensurate with our technological abilities in physical affairs.

This then is the task indicated. It is, if we employ large terms, to humanize science. This task in the concrete cannot be accomplished save as the fruit of science which is named technology is also humanized. And the task can be executed in the concrete only as it is broken up into vital applications of intelligence in a multitude of fields to a vast diversity of problems so that science and technology may be rendered servants of the democratic hope and faith. The cause is capable of inspiring loyalty in thought and deed. But there has to be joined to aspiration and effort the formation of free wide-ranging trained attitudes of observation and understanding such as incorporate within themselves, as a matter so habitual as to be unconscious, the vital principles of scientific method. In this achievement science, education, and the democratic cause meet as one. May we be equal to the occasion. For it is our human problem, and if a solution is found, it will be through the medium of human desire, human understanding, and human endeavor.

2

DEMOCRACY AND EDUCATION

I: INTRODUCTION
Sidney Hook

T HE CONFERENCE on the Scientific Spirit and Democratic Faith has taken as the basic theme of its discussion the ideals, practices, and problems of education in the modern world. Our reasons for selecting this theme are many. First, there is the obvious fact of its timeliness and importance. This is reflected in the remarkable stir and ferment in educational circles throughout the country. Not for generations has interest been so keen. But this interest extends far beyond professional educational groups. Almost all the governments of the world, and especially our own, are drawing up blueprints for educational reconstruction, to be sure, with more attention to its physical and administrative aspects than to underlying philosophy. But not only governments are becoming acutely conscious of educational issues. Newspapers also have launched campaigns to influence instruction. Churches are beginning to eye the schools as a new territory into which to carry the doctrine of salvation. The military services are evaluating the work of the school in relation to what they conceive will be the needs and tasks of tomorrow. Large scale industry is making plans in which the schools, on the vocational and technological side, have a significant part. Even business—to use a term broad enough to cover the ubiquitous real-estate associations—has altered the character of its traditional interest in education. In the past, business has viewed education primarily from the standpoint of its bearings on the tax-rate. Now it is directly concerned not only with the costs of tax supported and tax exempt schools but with the *content* of the schooling. The estimable Mr. Eddie Rickenbacker, who regards himself as a spokesman for business, and who was an expert on how to handle labor, has now blossomed out as an expert on progressive education.

In short, education is today front page news.

This well-nigh universal interest in education, no matter how varied its sources and interest, is a healthy and encouraging sign. It is to be hoped that soon everybody will understand that education is everybody's interest.

There is a second and more important reason for our discussion of education. This flows from the very purposes to which the Conference on the Scientific Spirit and Democratic Faith is dedicated.

We believe that the scientific spirit is a pervasive intellectual temper that is not confined to a set of laboratory procedures, and that its rationale should be extended to all social areas and institutions. The school, next to the family, is the most important social institution for the transmission of culture from one generation to another. We therefore ask: to what extent *is* our school education imbued with the values of the scientific spirit, and to what extent should it be? How do these values find expression in the ideals, curriculums, and methods of current American education, and what are the obstacles to their larger fulfillment?

We recognize that there are other educational agencies besides the schools, notably the press and radio and cinema through which meanings are daily communicated to large masses of people. How can the values of the scientific spirit be brought to bear to make these agencies more genuine educational instruments?

We cannot, therefore, be concerned with the scientific spirit and be indifferent to the character of our education in any of its forms.

The relation between the democratic faith and education is just as plain and even more fundamental. It would be an exaggeration to say that all the problems of democracy are problems of education. But it is no exaggeration to say that the validity of the democratic faith depends on faith in the possibilities of education. Indeed, this is one way of defining the democratic faith. If I had to define the democratic faith in one sentence I would say that it is a faith that through education men can become sufficiently reasonable to discover, in the face of evidence and the give and take of free discussion, a better way of solving their common problems than through any other process. We have not adequately explored what our faith in democracy means today until we have explored the basic problems of the education of our times.

A third reason for our concern with the theme of education broaches the subject of this section of our discussion. The Conference was organized, among other purposes, to combat a growing trend towards authoritarianism in the life of mind. In our previous discussions we examined critically the false doctrine that only a belief in supernatural revelation can serve as a proper foundation for the democratic way of life, and the pernicious corollary that therefore all humanists and naturalists are theoretical fellow-travellers of totalitarianism. To those who held this doctrine and its corollary, not Hitler, not Mussolini, not Franco, and the Argentinian Camarilla were the chief enemies of American democracy, but those whose morality depends for its sanctions upon its beneficent fruits in social and personal life. The same authoritarian tendency is at work in education. A long list of writers, more or less well-organized, and exercising an enormous influence on public opinion, have launched similar attacks against democratic humanism and naturalism in education. They charge that insofar as the educational philosophy behind American ideals, practices, and proposed reforms in education is not based on the true theology or the true metaphysics, it is in principle indistinguishable from Hitlerism. Among these writers, I list Monsignor Sheen, Robert Hutchins, the Rev. Robert I. Gannon, Stringfellow Barr, Thomas Woodlock, Mortimer Adler, and many others.

A typical expression of the line of attack by these men against philosophies of education that are rooted in humanist and naturalist world views is provided by Mr. Thomas Woodlock who writes in the *Wall Street Journal* of March 31, 1944, as follows:

This philosophy (underlying progressive education) amounts to a complete, detailed, formal denial of the fundamental principles upon which our nation was founded because it is completely totalitarian. In this respect it differs in no essential from the "philosophy" of Nazism, Fascism and Communism, and is fully as dangerous to the freedom of the human person.

This citation can be matched with passages from the writings of other individuals of this school. It is a view promulgated in a series of coast-to-coast broadcasts last winter by the so-called *Education for Freedom, Inc.* in cooperation with the Mutual Broadcasting System.

The Conference on the Scientific Spirit and Democratic Faith is not committed to any specific philosophy of education—be it progressive or conventional. It is committed only to free inquiry into the educational implication of both scientific method and democracy. In this inquiry, it becomes necessary to meet the challenge to free minds by those who believe that science, democracy, and education—all three—must get their directions from supernatural religious beliefs.

II: TRADITION AND TRADITIONALISTS

Arthur E. Murphy

No PHASE OF ITS PRESENT ACTIVITY should properly be of greater concern to a civilized community than the way in which it appropriates the past out of which it has developed. That usable past has been continued into the present as tradition and is embodied not only in venerated cultural monuments, but also, and more deeply, in the habits, preconceptions, and loyalties which are as much a part of the contemporary community, as a going concern, as are its material resources. The use it is able to make of this tradition will determine to a very considerable degree the range and level of its response to the demands of present action and to the promise and possibilities of the future. And since it is chiefly through education that the resources of the past are incorporated in the experience of each new generation, it is obvious that a good education is at least one that enables its possessor to make intelligent and responsible present use of the traditions of the community in whose life he shares.

There are, however, radical differences of opinion as to the way in which a tradition should function in the education of those who must, in the present and future, make the most of their own lives and contribute effectively to the life of their community. One such opinion, currently presented by its protagonists as a philosophy of education, can usefully be designated as "traditionalism." By "traditionalism" I shall hereafter mean that educational theory which holds that what it identifies as "our tradition" has provided us with a body of established truth about human nature, human values, and human destiny by reference to which currently unsettled questions of the correctness of beliefs, the rightness of actions and policies, and the excellence of works of art should be decided. The reverence and loyalty we owe to great men and great books for their contribution to our spiritual heritage are, in this philosophy, transmuted into a present authority supposed to be possessed by their doctrines as information about man and the world and by their valuations as disclosures of eternal beauty and goodness. To educate the rising generation to a proper appreciation of "our tradition," then, means to indoctrinate it in views on these high matters which have come down to us in books that are landmarks in our cultural history and which the traditionalist asks us to accept in consequence as present gospel for an erring world. The traditionalists believe this gospel to be right and reasonable, but they are not prepared to rest the case for it on its own presently ascertainable merits. Preferring instead to appear as "the ghosts of departed wisdom," their method is to ask us to consider now disputed questions as they appeared at a selected period in the past to the best minds of that time, and to accept the conclusions then reached, and now enshrined in the best books of "our tradition," as authoritative expressions of the wisdom, goodness, and essential content of all properly liberal education.

Explicitly stated, such a theory is hardly impressive and it is therefore a normal part of the campaign in its favor to avoid such explicit statement and to discourse instead of the tautologically eternal first principles and the academically venerable great books from which this questionable educational philosophy seeks to borrow a needed intellectual prestige. Confused but well-meaning people are often imposed on by this procedure and the traditionalists' cause acquires in their minds that kind of vacuous pseudo-profundity which is the current cut-rate substitute for philosophic wisdom. Hence, in the interest of philosophic clarity and responsible thinking, it will be worth our while to examine the most recent version of traditionalism with some care and to see it for what it is. The decision as to its philosophic and educational merits, once this operation is completed, will not be difficult to reach.

This philosophy has recently appeared under various titles, and with a variety of slogans. It is perhaps best known at present as the recovery of the liberal arts by the reading of 100 great books at St. John's College, as "Education for Freedom," over the Mutual Broadcasting System, and as the spiritual revolution which has for some years been incubating at the University of Chicago. President Hutchins of that University has effectively combined all these slogans, and others as well, in his own variety of educational philosophy and it is to his writings and those of his associates at Chicago and St. John's that we can properly turn for its elucidation.

In *Education for Freedom* Dr. Hutchins tells us that

> the liberal arts are the arts of freedom. To be free a man must understand the tradition in which he lives. A great book is one that yields up through the liberal arts a clear and important understanding of our tradition. An education which consists of the liberal arts as understood through great books and of great books as understood through the liberal arts would be one and the only one which would enable us to understand the tradition in which we live. It must follow that if we want to educate our students for freedom, we must educate them in the liberal arts and in the great books.[1]

1. Robert M. Hutchins, *Education for Freedom*, Baton Rouge: Louisiana State University Press, p. 14.

If this seems as vague as it is logically loose, further specification is by no means wanting. The great books, the fine flower of the great tradition of our Western Culture, are just 100 in number and they comprise the total curriculum of St. John's College where everybody reads them all. As for the liberal arts, Dr. Mark Van Doren, who appears to speak with authority for this group, has been most explicit. "What are the liberal arts by name? Tradition, grounded in more than two millenniums of intellectual history, calls them grammar, rhetoric and logic; arithmetic, music, geometry and astronomy."[2] "Latin Europe" called the first three the trivium and the last four the quadrivium. Some latitude may be permitted in their teaching, but there can be no deviation as to essentials. "The educator by tradition is a liberal artist who knows his seven disciplines and imposes them upon the pupil who comes to him. Tradition licenses him to be lopsided, to favor this order or that. But there are seven items which he orders, and he knows their names. Without their names the contemporary teacher is either a pretender or a specialist."[3]

There is, however, more to the proposal than this, and those who have dismissed it as a mere stunt in curriculum-making have done its authors a grave injustice. It is, in fact, to be the first step in a spiritual revolution— "the moral, intellectual and spiritual reformation for which the world waits," and which, as Dr. Hutchins tells us

> depends . . . upon true and deeply held convictions about the nature of man, the ends of life, the purposes of the state, and the order of goods. One cannot take part in this revolution if one believes that men are no different from the brutes, that morals are another name for the mores, that freedom is doing what you please, that everything is a matter of opinion, and that the test of truth is immediate practical success. . . . The revolution to which we are called must end in the destruction of these notions and their power over individual and political action.[4]

Now these objectionable doctrines are not merely current at the present time; if Dr. Hutchins is to be believed, they are rampant in American education. There are "cults" of skepticism, presentism, scientism, anti-intellectualism, and materialism at work, and materialism is even said to have "captured" our culture, the state and education.[5] Hence, the revolution must be drastic, and the reversal of the beliefs now common in our colleges and universities very radical indeed. Yet all this can be initiated by "one

2. Mark Van Doren, *Liberal Education*, New York: Henry Holt & Co., p. 85.
3. *Ibid.*
4. *Education for Freedom*, page 47.
5. *Ibid.*, page 42.

college and one univeṙsity" which will return to the liberal arts and the
great books and teach them as they should be taught. It is obvious, therefore, that the teaching in question is intended to lead students not merely
to understand "our tradition" but also to embrace certain doctrines derived from it which Dr. Hutchins regards as the creedal prerequisites for
his proposed reformation and to reject (and finally to "destroy") others
which are set down as objectionable.

This, evidently, is education for freedom in still a further sense. Under
such a system, if it is to achieve its revolutionary objective, the student will
no longer be free, as he is at present, to imbibe the doctrines of the heretical
cults which it is a major aim of the reformation to destroy. But what of
that? "The mind cannot be free if it is enslaved to what is good. To determine the good and the order of goods is the prime object of all moral and
political education."[6] The language is instructive, as was that of Dr. Van
Doren's in his description of the educator as the liberal artist who "imposes" his seven disciplines upon his pupils, with only that leeway and lop-
sidedness in which he is licensed by the tradition of two millenniums to indulge. We may sum the matter up by saying that the student who is truly
educated for freedom is to be enslaved to the good and the order of goods
as established through a properly disciplined interpretation of selected
classics whose high place in "our tradition" is supposed to establish their
authority as sources of contemporary knowledge and insight. And this is
to be done by "arts" whose names have been established "by tradition"
over two millenniums and for which, as Van Doren assures us, "no new
names have been found."[7] "Education for freedom" thus becomes the current alias for traditionalism, and freedom itself is bondage to the good
which a traditionally correct study of the classics is relied upon to disclose.

Such a proposal may at first have an odd sound to many of us, who have
lacked the benefit of the new liberal education, but that, after all, is not surprising. For as Professor John U. Nef, an ardent Hutchins disciple, has
pointed out in a remarkable book, culture in America is now on a very low
level indeed. We seem to have lost all respect for authority in matters
moral, intellectual, and artistic. "Who today," he asks with some bitterness,
"would think of condemning an erring husband or wife for unfaithfulness
by citing Aristotle?"[8] It is a question which might well give us pause. I am
not sure that the particular instance is well selected. Family life in ancient
Athens was rather different from our own and the picture of Aristotle as
the Dr. Anthony of the new spiritual reformation has its humorous side.

6. *Education for Freedom*, page 91.
7. *Liberal Education*, page 81.
8. John U. Nef, *The United States and Civilization*, Chicago: University of Chicago Press,
p. 117.

But a modest reformulation will put the question in proper historical perspective. "Who today would think of condemning erring reformers who advocate the abolition of human slavery by citing Aristotle?" Not many, perhaps, for the Age of Reason and the liberal 19th century have undermined the "authority" of some of the "unkillable classics" on this important issue. Yet in the ages that are "by tradition" great and whose version of the liberal arts is particularly venerated by Professor Nef and his associates, Aristotle passed for a great authority on just this subject, and the citation of his views of human nature, of the principles of government, and of the order of goods was held to be especially cogent in this connection. If we no longer believe that such citations provide sufficient "authority" for the justification of slavery it is not altogether because our education in the classics has been neglected. It is partly because we have learned in the meantime something about the order of values proper to a free society which Aristotle never understood. This does not mean that we now have nothing to learn from Aristotle. What it does mean is that what we can learn from him, or from any other great man long dead, is properly to be determined not by the citation of authoritative texts, but by independent, responsible *present* judgment on the merits of the issues with which we, and not our ancestors, are called upon to deal. If Aristotle's doctrines are pertinent to these issues and if they will stand inspection in the light of the widest experience now available, then they deserve our acceptance not bcause they are traditional but because they are true. It is truth, not tradition, that makes men free, and while they can find in the traditionally admired masterpieces of art, science, and philosophy much that is both true and pertinent, they will never know it when they see it, or how to distinguish it from what is no less traditional and false, if their "education for freedom" has taught them to defer to that tradition as an authority rather than to use it as a resource and point of departure for the work which only the present can do and the decisions which free men make on their own authority.

Walter Lippmann, who shares the St. John's zeal to derive from cultural tradition the doctrinally authoritative content of contemporary teaching, reminds us in a recent essay[9] of the saying of Bernard of Chartres that the men of any generation are like dwarfs seated on the shoulders of giants. The moral is that we must conserve our tradition if we are to progress. But it is one thing to be seated on the shoulders of the ancients, using the height thus attained to see further than they have seen, and another to be prostrate at their feet, piously invoking the limitations of their necessarily

9. "Man in American Education." Now reprinted in *Democracy: Should It Survive?* Milwaukee: Bruce Publishing Co., pp. 49-58.

limited standpoint as the canons for right thinking on the eternal verities. Even dwarfs, who are often very intelligent, should surely know better than to confuse the latter procedure with the former.

The emptiness of the traditionalist "reformation" becomes apparent as soon as one begins to inquire seriously what the authoritative doctrine is that the contemporary student is to imbibe from the 100 best books. Dr. Hutchins seems to be confident that the study of just these books will be a potent agent in the destruction of the doctrines of which he disapproves. One such is "skepticism." Yet among the unkillable classics in the St. John's curriculum are Montaigne, Gibbon, Voltaire, Hume, and Poincaré. Is their authority to be invoked on this matter? Will the liberally educated student learn from Kant's *Critique of Pure Reason* that respect for metaphysics which the traditionalists are so eager to inspire? Will he find in Bacon, Galileo, Descartes, Spinoza, and Bentham the needed corrective to contemporary "scientism," or in Machiavelli, Hobbes, and Hegel the principles of political morality which Dr. Hutchins holds to be essential for the vindication of democracy? If "our tradition" is summed up in the 100 books in the St. John's curriculum then our tradition, as represented by Rousseau, Freud, and William James, lays the foundation for just the sort of anti-intellectualism that the traditionalists denounce. And so it is on all the major issues. Plato, Calvin, Rabelais, Swift, Tolstoy, Marx, and John Stuart Mill (all in the canon) have important things to say about the "nature of man, the ends of life and the order of goods," but to suppose that what can be extracted from their teachings by a judicious use of grammar, rhetoric, and logic, or even of arithmetic, music, geometry, and astronomy, adds up to an authoritative verdict of "our tradition" on these matters is preposterous.

The truth is, of course, that the works that make up "the great tradition" as an academically reputable selection of masterpieces in literature, science, and philosophy simply do not constitute a tradition at all in the sense of an authoritatively agreed on body of doctrine in terms of which contemporary heresies can be put down. The great writings of the past which constitute our intellectual heritage were not collections of beautiful sayings designed to dwell peacefully side by side in anthologies or provide the nobly articulated slogans for a twentieth century indoctrination in 13th century modes of thought. They were the sometimes twisted, often angry and one-sided, always human and hence provisional strivings of men of genius to make the most of the world as they saw it. Because they saw it with greater directness, or deeper penetration, or broader understanding than had their predecessors and contemporaries, they carried forward at some points and in some measure the great enterprise to which they were devoted—the endlessly precarious, endlessly controversial, and endlessly rewarding enterprise of human enlightenment. It is one of the sillier aspects of traditionalism that it asks us to venerate the intellectual heroes of our tradition neither as they were when they were alive, in the uncertain, courageous, fighting span of experience that was their present, nor as they would be if they were alive today, sharing with us in the work of our present and helping solve its problems, but as cultural remains transformed by their now respectable antiquity into disclosures of timeless truth. It was not thus that these masterpieces were created, nor thus that they can effectively be appropriated by a generation worthy to continue for itself the enterprise to which the great men of the past so greatly contributed. And so, to put it bluntly, this great tradition, viewed as the choir of departed sages hymning in harmony those eternal principles of wisdom and goodness which are to provide at once the inescapable content of an accelerated A.B. degree and the slogans of a nearly scholastic spiritual revolution is a fake, and whosoever is deceived thereby is not wise.

If we could be quite sure that it was simply to a "tradition" of this academic and attenuated sort that the traditionalists were appealing, we could reasonably regard their effort as misguided and wasteful of time and ingenuity that might have been expended in a better cause, but hardly as a serious challenge to our American system of free secular education. There is, however, a much narrower sort of tradition to which they sometimes appeal and which is, for purposes of authoritarian indoctrination in eternal first principles, of a considerably more formidable character. This is not a doctrine to be gleaned from all the 100 best books, or even from the majority of them, but exclusively from those which teach an approved theological theory about the supernatural origin of man and the supernatural validation of his political rights. This theory holds that men possess the human dignity which justifies their claim to freedom as an "ancestral appanage" or supernatural endowment. And it is further maintained that without the acceptance of this doctrine the case for political democracy cannot "ultimately" be made out or faith in it maintained. At this point the campaign for "education for freedom" becomes explicitly a demand for theological orthodoxy as a prerequisite for political loyalty and political unity in the cause of freedom.[10]

That the proposed return to orthodoxy would require something in the nature of a purge, or purification, of many theories now current in our schools and colleges is fairly clear. We should expect that "scientism" and its related heresies would not fare well under such a régime. But M. Mari-

10. This view is strongly stated by Mr. Thomas F. Woodlock in his foreword to *Democracy: Should It Survive?*

tain, whose teachings our American traditionalists regard with the greatest respect, has recently pointed out that we must go much further back than that. Democracy, he tells us, is threatened by dangerous ideological enemies.

> If its root is evangelical, if it stems from that movement of hidden stimulation by means of which Christianity dimly activates earthly history, it is nonetheless by aligning itself with erroneous ideologies and misguided tendencies that it made its appearance in the world. Neither Locke, nor Jean-Jacques Rousseau, nor the Encyclopedists can pass as thinkers faithful to the integrity of the Christian heritage. There, too, everything indicates that a great renewal of the spirit is being prepared, which tends to bring democracy back to its true essence and purify its principles.[11]

Now this is surely a very remakable statement. If the Encyclopedists are to be excluded from the heritage from which our democracy can draw its inspiration, Thomas Jefferson must certainly go with them, for on matters theological he shared their views, and was bitterly attacked in this country for so doing. If the author of "The Confession of Faith of the Savoyard Vicar" is unacceptable, what is to be said of Emerson or William James or for that matter of two-thirds of the liberal theologians of our own time? What is to be said of John Dewey, America's greatest living philosopher, we already know, for the more outspoken of the traditionalists have told us.[12] And if John Locke, whose *Treatises on Civil Government* were the political Bible of the American Revolution, whose *Reasonableness of Christianity* is a model of Protestant piety, and whose *Letter Concerning Toleration* ranks among the greatest defenses of freedom ever written, is taboo, then it is hard to know who, among the actual authors of our faith in freedom, will survive. Certainly not John Milton or Roger Williams or Tom Paine. Indeed, as M. Maritain makes clear, it was on its first appearance in the world that democracy aligned itself with erroneous and misguided tendencies, and it is to be expected, therefore, that to regain the required purity of principles we shall have to return intellectually to an era in which democracy had not emerged at all, an era in which the supernaturally guaranteed dignity of man was authoritatively held to be fully compatible with his political subjugation, and with the denial of freedom of teaching to all those outside the boundaries of the established church. It is at least remarkable that it is just where it has thus aligned itself with the "errors" of "misguided" men that democracy has managed to establish in

11. *Ibid.,* page 146.
12. See, for example, Mr. Woodlock's observations in *op. cit.,* page 8.

fact the kind of freedom to which the traditionalists are, in principle, so profoundly attached.

It is important to be clear as to the issue for *educational policy* which this doctrine has actually raised. There is no reason why M. Maritain should not disapprove of Locke and Rousseau, or of Jefferson and William James, if he chooses, or why Mr. Woodlock should conceal his evident antipathy for the philosophy of John Dewey. What is important—and alarming—is the claim that the acceptance of these beliefs is necessary for *political purposes* (as "education for freedom" in the sense in which this country is committed to its maintenance and defense) and hence can properly be demanded of those who teach and are taught in our schools ánd colleges, not on the ground of the independently ascertainable truth of the beliefs in question—about which some competent inquirers might disagree—but as the required ideological "foundation" for our democracy. There are various pretexts on which such a philosophy might be advanced, but the oddest of all of them, in this country, is the one that has actually been selected, the appeal to tradition and the wisdom of the past. For the plain fact is that in this country we have got a tradition of freedom—strong, persistent, and deeply-rooted—that is profoundly opposed to the whole "traditionalist" procedure, and on this point explicitly so. Perhaps this tradition has not been clearly understood by the authoritarian reformers. Some of them are but recently arrived in this country and others, like Dr. Hutchins, have frequently complained of the inadequacy of their education in spiritual fundamentals. It may, therefore, be worth our while to point out, to those who did not know or have forgotten, the nature of this tradition and the reasons why we honor and defend it.

It is a tradition that goes a long way back and that owes a debt we would never disavow to the faith and philosophy of the 13th century. But it did not stop growing in that century, or in those that followed. It came to America in the 17th century in the fighting faith of religious sects whose members wanted a guarantee of freedom not only in principle but in practice and who knew how to secure it for themselves. They learned here, after the bitterest sort of controversy, that, in a country that is effectively free, religious toleration must be an equal right for all, and that a sect which claims such toleration for its teaching is obligated to accord it to others, even when it might, by appeal to the secular arm, secure a spiritual and educational monopoly for its own doctrines. This has long seemed to us, in America, a considerable advance in that ideal of equal freedom and fair dealing which is a part of our tradition. And so long as we retain it we are not likely to look with favor on the claims of groups or sects that seek to engross the spiritual foundations, ideological content, and educational ideals of democracy as their own exclusive property.

The 18th century, too—the Age of Reason—had something distinctive to contribute to this tradition of freedom. The men who wrote the Declaration of Independence and the Constitution had in many instances the benefit of a good classical education, as traditionalists like to remind us, but when they undertook to say what political freedom was to mean in this country it was not as traditionalists that they spoke. One of their most striking contributions to the practice of freedom was precisely that "secularism" or separation of church and state, set down as the first item in the first article of the Bill of Rights, which authoritarians in politics and in education have always viewed with alarm. The emancipation of political allegiance from all tests of theological orthodoxy, and the recognition that men may differ in their religious views without prejudice to their status as sharers in the faith and freedom of a democratic community, have since that time been very much a part of our tradition. It may seem trite at this point to refer to the teachings of Thomas Jefferson, but since none of his writings are included in the "best books" at St. John's, it is perhaps advisable to remind our traditionalists of their pertinence to this issue and to suggest that those who wish to instruct their students in the meaning of free institutions would be well advised to consult them. For if we are really going to return to "our" tradition in these high matters it is surely of particular importance to see that the tradition in question is authentic, and our own.

The 19th century is not looked upon with much favor by lovers of the antiquities, but it was a great period in the growth of free institutions. It was the century in which the "rights" eternally guaranteed to "Man" by his supernatural derivation were progressively extended, in countries where "liberalism" was a political ideal and not a term of reproach, to those men who do the ordinary work of the world, and in which slavery was largely abolished, the organization of workers for the furtherance of their economic interests developed, and free secular education extended to those classes whose spiritual welfare had previously been supposed by no means to require it. It is to be expected that when quite common people win for the first time the means of satisfying their desires in their own way, they will show themselves to be crude and, from the standpoint of the élite, materialistic. For "materialism" is very often the name given by refined critics to the demand for a larger share in this world's goods by those whose self-interest has not as yet been hallowed by the cultural proprieties. Professor Nef is grieved at the spectacle of masses of Americans seeking comfort, security, and self-expression in activities in which the workers of the

13th century were in no position to indulge. They are indeed by no means so thoroughly "enslaved to the good" as their predecessors. Indeed, in some important phases of their lives, they are no longer enslaved at all. And they crudely tend to believe that this is good—a fulfillment rather than an ideological distortion of their democratic heritage.

Yet the 19th century in America was not without its spiritual prophets. No men ever combatted the preoccupation of their countrymen with *merely* material goods more courageously or explicitly than Emerson, Theodore Parker, and Thoreau. They were learned men for their time and they had profited from their study of the classics. But when they spoke for the ideal of spiritual excellence which they believed to be possible to human nature it was not in the name of an "authority" derived from a pious picking over of the literary remains of a borrowed culture. They spoke as men who could judge for themselves and in their own day the things that are good and find in them, for those with eyes to see, the promise of more day that is yet to dawn. For them the spiritual, as Emerson said, is that which is its own evidence, and the Americans who are to discern it will be those who can stand on their own feet and speak their own minds. It is a pity there was no room for *Walden,* or the *American Scholar,* or *Leaves of Grass* among the "unkillable classics" at St. John's. There is a native tang to them and a native integrity from which an understanding of our tradition could profit much and for which no amount of undergraduate study of Plotinus (in translation) is likely to serve as an adequate substitute.

Nor did the tradition of freedom cease to grow as we came into the 20th century. The years of the reform era, of the "new freedom," new poetry, and even new realism, were among the best in our history. The term "progressive," in those days had a genuinely constructive meaning, for we were learning the social responsibilities of our individualism and beginning, though still in a very tentative way, to translate what we learned into a program for action. John Dewey's *Democracy and Education* spoke for that period at its best and its teachings have been woven deeply into the texture of American thought and practice.

And so it is that when the apostles of the St. John's gospel tell us that we must now by drastic methods acquire a tradition if we are to preserve our democracy, we are not greatly impressed. We have a tradition, and there is great health and sanity in it and a capacity for growth that has by no means yet been exhausted. Perhaps they thought we did not care about it because we have not come forward to demand that authoritative formulations of its principles be imposed on every one as the required doctrinal content of all liberal education. But that, as it happens, is not a way in which our tradition has so far found it necessary to maintain itself. We still tend to believe, with Tom Paine, that given a fair field and no favors "Reason, like time, will make its own way," and we think it particularly important that it be permitted to do so in institutions of higher learning in which the ideals of freedom must be not only preached but practised if they are to win the credence and respect of intelligent men. We realize that this tradition has its limitations, and that it must continue to grow and develop if, in our own time, we are to be adequate to the great unfinished tasks remaining before us. And it is for that reason that we cannot regard any past formulation, however great, as the measure to which all further development must conform. This will no doubt seem a mark of weakness to those who wish to use tradition as a censor, or a crutch, or a cultural refuge from the crudities and responsibilities of contemporary life. But in our tradition the men we rightly honor have not found it so. They have found it instead a source of renewed vitality for the new effort and new achievement which continue in the present and into the future the enterprise by which effective freedom is won anew, as it must be, in every generation. Thus, in a tradition we still honor and to which, by something much deeper than a college course in the "unkillable classics," we are committed, we are not traditionalists.

This does not mean, however, that we can afford to feel at ease about American education, or rest on the laurels of Thomas Jefferson or John Dewey. We have our own work to do, of the most challenging and exacting sort. How can we develop the ideals of tolerance, which have enabled us to unite men of different religious beliefs in a single nation to the point at which we can cooperate, in an international order, with nations whose economic systems and political traditions differ radically from our own? This cooperation is needed urgently, not 500 years from now, but in the difficult times that will follow this war. How can we bring all aspects of human experience within the scope of rational inquiry in such a way that the "reason" we employ will be an adequate instrument for the understanding and evaluation of the issues of life, not an excuse for a one-sided emphasis on those disciplines so far officially accredited as "scientific" in their content and methods? How can we so enlighten the "practicalism" which seems a part of our native way of thinking as to make it clear that effective practice is concerned as much with ends as with instruments and that no ends are good enough that require for their attainment less than the best of which we are capable?

These are questions that must be answered if the wisdom and goodness which, as Dr. Hutchins reminds us, are the goals of education are to be translated from the plane of pious tautology and cultural reminiscence to

that of enlightened action. We do not know all the answers yet, being in
this respect less fortunate than some of the traditionalists, and even when
we get them, there will be still more questions. But we have learned
enough, from tradition and experience, to be reasonably assured that in
the process of finding answers to such problems there is enough to learn
and to achieve to keep both us and our students very profitably at work and
to further, in ways beyond our present calculation, the actualization of
those spiritual values in which the enterprise of human understanding
finds its appropriate and adequate fulfilment.

III: THE ARTS OF LIBERATION
Irwin Edman

W AR, for all its tragedy and train of disorders, forces a reconsideration
of fundamentals. It is not surprising that liberal education should
have come in for the most intense discussion at the very moment when it
is in large measure being suspended. Educators bereft of pupils and even
of plans have asked themselves often for the first time in many years, what
they are doing; they have asked themselves particularly with respect to the
liberal arts, to education in which as in no other country in the world
American youth has been exposed. The routine of American education, the
stereotype textbooks, the empty routine of campus social life, the lack of a
serious sense of the great humane tradition of the past, all this has long
worried educators. In the 18th century men like Thomas Jefferson in this
country, had, along with a vivid sense of a new future on a new continent,
a profound sense of the heritage of the great tradition. In American colleges it has sometimes seemed as if the proliferation of new subjects, new
courses, new methods, the concern for the individual temperament of the
student, the desire to be up-to-date, has destroyed the depths and range of
the old classical curriculum.

In the face of the collapse of the liberal arts curriculum of mathematics
and the classics, a new solution has been suggested. We have heard over
and over again in the last ten years about the great books. We have been
asked to revive the liberal arts by reviving a study of the great books in the
Western tradition particularly. The argument hardly needs recapitulation.
It is the doctrine of the great books as a solution that needs criticism.

Broadly speaking there are two general reasons for reviving the study of the great books of the past. They are stimulating and enriching works of art. They speak to all men everywhere. Homer's radiant and fresh world is open to us in the twentieth century by the art of a poetry that transcends the time and place of its birth. The drama of Greece and the poetry of Dante, the philosophical dialogues of Plato and the plays of Shakespeare, these are good any time anywhere. They speak with an eloquence, clarity, and persuasiveness unmatched by lesser books of their own time or of *our* own. Secondly, they are our common heritage. They have rendered the thought, language, and emotions of mankind in a way that enables us to speak a common language and to understand each other, to be friends in the same country of the mind. They are the voices of the spirit of man in its diverse and recurrent aspects. They are the language of the conscience, thought, and imagination of the human race.

All this is true. It is also true that American colleges have tended to forget it. They have read textbooks about books. They have generated new pseudo-sciences, and jargons of pretentious up-to-dateness. They have substituted elaborate gadgets and methodologies for the life blood of great books. They have tried to vie with the newspapers and the movies and the radios. They have given up the patrimony of the past, the liberation that comes from initiation to a tradition larger and wider than our own era. In this sense the call back to the great books is a challenge, and incidentally one that had not gone unheeded, long before St. Johns College was thought of and thunder blasted from the University of Chicago. At Columbia College in New York, for more than a quarter of a century, a study of the great books of the European tradition has been a signal part of the curriculum. But not the whole of it. For there is as great a danger in thinking that the reading of a number of masterpieces in the humanistic fields of philosophy and literature or even of past science, is the whole of a liberal education. The whole meaning of liberal education is lost unless the sense of liberation is kept in the word. Great works of art, in any art, music and painting, as well as literature liberate the spirit of man. They are instruments by which he learns to feel with clarity and intensity, to see and to hear. Education is designed to render men at once disciplined and free, disciplined to understand the nature of the world and the society in which they live, free by their competence and discrimination and range of feeling and thought to make intelligent choices.

For this there is no question that the masterpieces of European literature and of the East are great resources. They embody in the accent of genius the distinct voices in which the human spirit has spoken at various periods and in various contexts of human history. But these books are not the only instruments of imagination and understanding. Nor are they liberating to the spirit of men in our time if they are approached as if they were a set of sacred and finished doctrines to be taught as final repositories of wisdom. Books mean different things at different times to different generations and even in the same generation to different students with different vocations, capacities, temperaments, and destinies. They are not strait-jackets to be worn but experiences to be mastered diversely by different students at different times. Nor are these great books instruments of understanding if they are studied as if they were written in vacuo and were addressed to no generation in particular. The dialogues of Plato were written by an Athenian writing out of the context of a given society and written with the audience of that society in mind. Dante was a child of the Middle Ages and Goethe of the eighteenth century.

Nor are they understood when they are separated from the other arts and from the sciences of their day. Dante is filled with the learning of his time and Shakespeare with the world that was being explored and thought about by pioneers and scientists as well as by poets. The music and art of the 18th century is an adjunct, and an important one, to the understanding of the books of that era. And the books are to be understood finally, obviously, by students of our own time with its own problems and its own, often new, intellectual resources. In a basic sense we live in the present and toward the future, and the only importance of the past is that it lives and helps to live richly in the present and wisely toward the future. It is a new and narrow scholasticism to assume that the study of the books of the past is the whole of a liberal education. Aristotle, as has been repeatedly pointed out, had no Aristotle before him. He looked at the world with a steady and candid eye. He did not keep his eyes on a revered classic, an old orthodoxy of thought.

Since the beginning of the modern period the sciences have opened up a vast new avenue to human understanding. They have been looked on with scorn by those enamored of a purely literary education. But there is an enormous accession to the freedom and dignity of man in learning the method of responsible inquiry by which man has learned to control his physical resources and may be expected eventually to control his social and spiritual environment. In the same way there has grown up of necessity in a modern, technical, complicated, industrial society, an enormous number of new vocations and professions.

The older literary education scorned not only the sciences; it scorned the professions, the vocations, and the trades. As a result liberal culture has been the thin after-image of the culture of the past, a gloss and veneer of classical allusion and a mouthing of the politenesses of a genteel culture. Meanwhile, there has grown up an enormous flourishing active vocational education. Some of the best teaching in this country has taken place in first-rate engineering schools. But that education has tended to become not education but specialized training. There has been a tragic divorce in our society between the genteel education originally intended for a leisure class, and a technical training designed for *ad hoc* experts, prepared to do the complex technical jobs of a modern industrial and mechanical society.

The results have been disastrous for our world. Scientific training has meant a class of purely mechanical experts. Liberal culture has meant a class devoted to the traditions of the past. Culture has become empty and backward-looking; technical training has had no vision at all. There is no question that the culture of the whole man in the serious sense of that'word is the business of education as opposed to special training. But the culture of the whole man does not come from a backward exploration of books however great, or arts however moving. Young men and young women are being educated here and now. Great books grew out of great and living societies; the great arts grew out of the living interests and concerns of living men. The Cathedral of Chartres was not a monument to be looked at as a memento of culture but as an expression of the living aspirations of living men. Insofar as books are living now they are worth studying. But there are other things worth studying as well, for the discipline of the mind and imagination of students in our time.

And even these things are worth studying because they help us to see more clearly, vividly, and intently what it is to live in the present, what it is to hope and dream for and plan for the future.

It is, therefore, no liberal education at all to study the great books, the great arts of the past only as monuments of the dead, and mausoleums in which the living can bury themselves in an irrelevant and marmoreal beauty. The great books, the great arts do not function at all educationally if they only function as escape, if they do not act as dynamic agents of a fresh approach to experience. They are worse than not liberal; they are chains if they become simply patterns on which we sentimentally try to reconstruct our own culture, seeking in vain and foolishly to achieve an alleged 13th century unity in our own day, to reconstruct our society in terms of a faith which is not expressive of its imagination or its problems, to attempt to make a polity resembling that of Plato's vision, a vision of Greek life, or to make in a twentieth century global civilization an imitation of the city-state of Athens or of Sparta.

Books and arts transcend their origins and there is no question that the great books, the great arts speak to men beyond the times and circumstances of their birth. The Elizabethan madrigals were born in a certain culture pattern but their beauty speaks to us in our modern day. Books and arts speak to us who live now, who face the future. We take from them what is relevant to us; we can take nothing else without pretense.

Meanwhile there are in the vast new possibilities and forms of knowledge of our own day hints, gleams, suggestions, perplexities, and problems which we cannot derive from a patrimony however splendid, or a culture of the past however beautiful. The methods of scientific inquiry have opened new worlds, and the method itself, relatively new, has opened domains of the human imagination, and new disciplines to thought hitherto untouched and undreamed of. The fruits of scientific method have, of course, been enormous in the way of comforts, gadgets, and ease in life, as well as means for its destruction. Science is popularly often conceived to be a palace of mechanical wonders or a chamber of mechanical horrors. But the fruits of science are spiritual and educative as well, and these are only beginning to be realized or broached in modern study and teaching. They have scarcely affected the imagination of the general educated public, or even the basic forms and assumptions of thought of scientists themselves. The very method of scientific inquiry is a moral lesson in objectivity, disinterestedness, and detachment. Its careful, patient procedure is a lesson in devotion and responsibility, respect for the facts as they are found to be, and faith in the infinite resources which understanding might make of nature for human uses. There is a whole making of a whole religion in the landscape of experience as inquiry discloses it, and the prospects for mankind that that landscape suggests.

In the late 19th century there was a good deal of nostalgic lament about science and scientific method. These were supposed to denude the world of value and render it bleak and alien. The furniture of our imagination was borrowed from a tradition in which modern science was unknown. Science itself was associated with techniques for material control or aggrandizement. We are only now beginning to appreciate the ways in which the method of scientific inquiry functions as an instrument not only of physical control but of intellectual understanding. In such understanding is as much liberal education, in such apprehension of the order of our basic condition of existence is as much cultivation, as in any works of literature and art. And those works themselves are illuminated for us by a cool and scrupulous analysis of their own methods and their own consequences.

In the same way the vocations and professions of modern society have their own disciplines, their own suggested meanings and values. Unless the professions of law, medicine, engineering; unless the vocations of farmer, mechanic, and business man, are seen in the light of their human uses, they are merely tools or mechanisms, merely avenues to gadgets or profits. Unless those trained in the work necessary in our civilization are educated to see these tasks in the light of their humane implications and their imaginative significance in our civilization, we shall be having most of our population merely trained robots, not men. The distinction, that some suggest ought to be tightly drawn, between liberal and vocational education, is socially an extremely dangerous one, and one as fatal as anything could be to the democratic process. It breeds the notion of two classes of society, a class of patricians with a sense of liberal values, and a class of technicians with no conception of meaning or value at all. If carried out, it would render our culture the thin procession of a small class of aesthetes or professional intellectuals, and allow the business and the leisure of the lives of everyone else to be meaningless and mechanical. Unless our professional and technical men are educated to see the human bearings of what they do, and our academic and literary people are educated to the cultural significance of the activities of the world in which they as well as every one else live, we shall have liberal arts that liberate no one. They will give no one the deeper liberty that comes with understanding the significances of the civilization in which we actually live, the portents of the future which that living world suggests.

By the same token, we need to guard against the tendency to disparage all literature and art of the present time as over against the great tradition. All great literature has been an expression of life, and every generation, though human nature remains substantially the same, has its own accents and its own problems, its own mood and its own temper. To concentrate exclusively on the great tradition is to forget that a great tradition is always in the making and in our generation here, among us. Posterity will winnow out our great books, but if we are to understand ourselves and our world, we need to read and study those serious efforts of poets to express, of novelists to depict, of painters to mirror, of music to sing in terms and accents of our own living awareness.

It is claimed, finally, that what our age misses, so vast is it and so miscellaneous, is what the great established canon of the past can provide. It is tragically true that our time is rent by disharmonies of which the war is the most spectacular instance. But unity is not arrived at by reviving a pattern of the Greeks or the medievals. It is to be arrived at by a gradual new synthesis incorporating the inherited values of our literary past with the values discovered in our present, in the world revealed by inquiry and celebrated by writers and thinkers aware of the new issues and new complexities of a global society, one whose fate and whose form are the expression and the foster child of scientific inquiry. The liberal arts include all those arts which discipline men to understand and challenge them to transform into a unity the vast complexities of the world we have, the people we are.

3

CAN FREE COMMUNICATION BE ACHIEVED?

I: INTRODUCTION
Harry D. Gideonse

WE TALK ABOUT THE FRUITS of education in terms of schools and formal education. We do not sufficiently stress the fact that a growing part of education today has no relation whatsoever with the institutions concerned with formal education. Several other agencies contribute in a marked way to the formation of human beings, young or adult. Two of the principal influences, of course, are the press and radio.

We tend to discuss young people still as if their education were an issue between, say, the church and the school, or from another angle as if it were an issue between the family and the school. A great deal of contemporary discussion of juvenile delinquency has run in terms of family responsibility as compared with school responsibility, but as anyone would recognize who thinks about it for just a moment, a very large part of the responsibility for the formation of young people today does not any longer rest in the school, at least as orthodoxly conceived, or in the family, whether orthodoxly conceived or not. It is exercised—responsibly or irresponsibly—by these other formative agencies.

The Regents' report in New York State made it emphatically clear statistically—and that seems to be the only clear truth that some people respect—that the average New York high-school youngster listens to radio from ten to fifteen hours a week. Without entering into a discussion as to what goes into the ten or fifteen hours, the bare fact shows you the relative importance—at least in terms of time—of, let us say, religious education, which reaches only a very limited group compared to the number reached by radio, and which certainly does not reach them for very much more than the one or one-and-one-half hour period that is typically devoted to religious education.

There is also the rôle of the so-called "comics," which together with news selection and emphasis, as well as the "educational" impact of the advertising pages, you can assign as a responsibility to the press.

We are in the habit of thinking of radicalism as over against conservatism in terms of problems of political or socio-economic organization; so-called free enterprise on the one hand, and controlled enterprise on the other. But if you think about the problems of a modern society like our own, it is difficult to avoid the conflicts between the motives that underlie family life and the demands of the material standard of living; and in the study of frustrated human drives you certainly will encounter before you have gone very far the influence of the systematic cultivation of material discontents which is exercised on its lowest common denominator level by the advertising specialist.

In this respect Henry David Thoreau was a far more radical critic of modern civilization than Karl Marx, because Karl Marx simply went along with the prevailing economism, with the prevailing emphasis on the material as related to the technological aspect of our culture, and built up what he thought were the implications of that kind of an economic, technical kind of culture if it followed what he considered its own law to its logical conclusion.

Thoreau asked very much more critical and therefore much more subversive questions about a society that based itself fundamentally in its economic and technical life on the assumption that human wants, economically speaking, were unlimited, and that progress was to be achieved by cultivating those unlimited wants.

Now that is, it seems to me, very near the core of the problem that we are discussing here. It is customary to discuss the problems of the press and of radio in terms of rather simple contrasts between white and black, in terms of freedom as over against government control. It is not customary to discuss these choices in terms of what we do—or might do—with the freedom or with the control.

If we are interested in a society that will be safe for cultural pluralism, we should not think of freedom and control as if they were black and white, but we should aim at an infinite variety, at a mosaic of kinds of grey that are subject to human modification and manipulation, and which allow through the mosaic of varying shades of grey corresponding degrees of freedom, depending upon the particular channel and the kind of cultural controls that have grown up around it.

That is very academic language. Still, it is the nearest that I can come to describing what I have in mind. Take, for instance, a recent issue of the *New York Times* with its story of Eddie Cantor's difficulties because somebody in one of the radio chains thought that something Cantor had per-petrated—or intended to perpetrate—on a television program was some-how likely to subvert somebody's morals.

Now, of course, it must be granted that a television program might sub-vert some people's morals. There is no issue about that, and I suppose all of us would agree that there must be some kind of safeguards at some level.

But it is also noteworthy that the agency that is likely to be the most vocal about moral safeguards, the church, in its various expressions is nowadays (for a church) remarkably singleminded in the things that it re-gards as immoral. There was a day when the church recognized seven categories of major sin, and the kind of sin that was related to sex, which, in the old days, was called luxury or lust, was only one of those seven. The others, like covetousness or pride or any of the other traditional forms—wrath being one of them, by the way—do not currently receive the emphasis which the church traditionally gave to them. Sometimes I think that pride and wrath are underemphasized because they are types of sin to which reli-gious folk are more likely to be vulnerable. But they are all sins in the orthodox theological catalogue of sins. Think of the emphasis on sex in contemporary moralizing, and then think of covetousness in relation, for instance, to modern advertising. Think of covetousness in relation to the basic assumption that a social order is only safe for democracy if it is built on an upward economic curve, which means a curve that assumes the in-finite increase of material wants. Now, that is just another way of saying that covetousness is one of the principal pillars of that society. In the per-spective of the traditional theological catalogue of sins, perhaps the moral-ist should pay some attention to the framework of the advertising appeal itself rather than spotlight the possible moral hazard involved in Eddie Cantor's hula-hula dancing for a television program.

Incidentally, this Eddie Cantor case may serve to illustrate what I said a moment ago concerning the mosaic of greys. Here is something that radio apparently thinks is morally subversive, and the *New York Times* comes along and prints the whole dialogue, word for word. The editor of the *Times* apparently thinks it will not hurt its thousands of readers, although the radio business thinks it may subvert the chap who has money enough to buy a television set.

I think it is good that we should have a situation surrounding the *Times* which makes it possible for it to run what Eddie Cantor was not allowed to show over television. I think it is terribly important that as we think our way through some kind of systematic way of handling and approaching these new problems, problems that emerge because new scientific techniques are made available, we do not yield too easily to the notion that the principles and the criteria and the incidence of control must be the same throughout. From the standpoint of the growing points in our culture, it is of the very essence of freedom to make it possible to preserve different levels of safeguards in the mosaic of cultural controls we set up. It is precisely that freedom to publish in the *Times* what was censored in television that keeps America a free society.

If we had a totalitarian control of communication, the brethren that kept Eddie Cantor's script off the air would also have kept it out of the newspaper. It may be a petty example, but it illustrates the main principle. Our safeguard there lay precisely in the fact that we had a diversity of controls.

Within a free system, the solution should be sought in the perfection of the design of the mosaic rather than in the elaboration of a uniform set of rules that will apply the same criteria of subversiveness in all the agencies of communication.

Our topic is "Can Free Communication be Achieved?" Perhaps that is too negative a statement. We have varying degrees and measures of freedom. "Can we improve the freedom of communication?" would to me be a better formulation of the problem as we have it.

II: PROBLEMS OF THE PRESS
Bruce Bliven

No one should need to argue the importance of the press in a democracy. The success of representative government depends upon the citizens being promptly, completely, and accurately informed; and the press is an essential tool for this purpose. The editors can exert an enormous influence, partly by writing editorials on one side or another of disputed public questions, but even more—in fact, ten times more—by coloring their news columns, and by suppressing or altering news items.

Many people are confused between honesty in the press and its cultural level. I find persons with whom I talk complaining in the same breath of journalism's dishonesty and of its vulgarity. Vulgarity is deplorable to those on a high cultural level, but it is far less important, in a society like ours, than honesty. In the United States, whose population represents all possible degrees of culture, education, and background, we shall undoubtedly for many decades to come require newspapers on varying levels of good taste, and it is pointless for the man with a Phi Beta Kappa key to object to the existence of newspapers intended primarily for cab drivers and sandhogs (and I hope that any Phi Beta Kappas who happen to be cab drivers or sandhogs will overlook the snobbishness of my statement).

Three great problems confront the American press at present. The problems are: winning the war, creating a durable peace, and creating and maintaining a high level of prosperity in the postwar period.

As to winning the war, the press on the whole is doing pretty well. I object to the incorrigible optimism which makes the newspapers portray the military situation every day as being better than in fact it is; and I object also when anti-administration newspapers, in order to hurt Mr. Roosevelt, make too much of the domestic hardships brought about by rationing and other war conditions. Nevertheless, the newspapers in general are undoubtedly filled with patriotic zeal and, on specific war questions, are trying loyally to cooperate with the directives from Washington.

As to the question of a durable peace, up to June, 1944, the press had ignored this subject almost entirely. Possibly the editors were waiting for the statesmen, who had also been laggard. (And possibly the statesmen had been waiting for the press to create a public demand for ideas.) Possibly the newspapers, most of them bitterly anti-Russian, could not bring themselves to face a world in which, obviously, the Russians will play an important part. It may be that Republican papers were waiting for a victory of their party in the election of November, 1944; it may be, again, that the editors feel advance planning of the postwar world is futile because events "just happen." I cannot believe that the editors have dodged the issue because they do not feel competent to give advice. I never knew an editor who did not feel entirely competent to tell his readers what ought to be done about all problems at all times.

On the third question, permanent postwar prosperity, the press up until June, 1944, had made an almost complete record of failure. Most competent economists believe that unless drastic steps are taken, we shall have after the war a short period of much prosperity and then a severe depression. But you find almost no hint of any such thing in the press, and no proposal except that we shall drop all wartime controls at the earliest possible moment and return to the conditions which existed from 1921 until 1929, the year in which began the worst depression in all history.

Why is this true? Several possible reasons can be seen. The American press is always over-optimistic, not merely about the shape of the war, as already mentioned, but on all subjects, at all times. In part, the editors believe—mistakenly, so far as I know—that optimism sells papers and pessimism does not. Possibly the editors are influenced here by their advertisers; advertising men are professional optimists, because they want you to buy everything in sight, whether you can afford it or not.

Undoubtedly, many editors, like many businessmen, sincerely believe in "free enterprise" and would not admit that it cannot solve all problems. They certainly would not now admit that free enterprise had the country in its grip from 1921 to 1929 and produced a complete breakdown, with the banks finally closed and 18,000,000 to 20,000,000 people out of work.

There is one other possible explanation of the attitude of certain newspaper editors. It is well known that some businessmen want a depression after the end of the war; they admit it privately, though publicly they are careful to avoid saying so. They think a short depression would "put labor in its place"—weaken the trade unions and deflate wages. I do not believe that many newspaper editors hold this view. I hasten to add that there are many businessmen who also repudiate it. They are the men who were badly frightened by what happened in this country when the depression was at its worst. They do not want a return to those conditions for fear they will bring on another New Deal, from their point of view as bad or worse than the first one.

In general, how is the press doing? Perhaps the one overwhelming fact about it is that it seems to be out of step with many of the most important movements in American life today. In the spring of 1944 we had additional evidence that this is true. The press reported an overwhelming tide of reaction against the New Deal throughout the country; yet primary elections in state after state seemed to indicate that the opposite was true; one New Dealer after another was chosen in the primaries over anti-New Deal candidates. The November election, which was still some months distant when this Conference took place, may show a different trend; but whether it does or not, there is no doubt that the newspapers of this country as a whole do not reflect the interests and desires of the people of this country as a whole. Public opinion polls show this to be true; so do earlier elections. The press represents the economic, financial, political, and cultural interests of a small minority which embraces most of the financial and economic power of the nation and includes the publishers themselves. Labor, the farmer, the white-collar worker, liberals, are all seriously under-represented in the press.

For a good illustration of this, I refer you to a careful study made by *The New Republic* following the election of 1936. We found that in the ten leading cities of the United States, 70 percent of the newspapers were against President Roosevelt. (I do not mean 70 percent of the number of papers, but 70 percent of their total combined circulations.) In those same cities 70 percent of the popular vote went to President Roosevelt. If I were the editor of one of these papers I should be seriously concerned to find that my readers paid so little attention to my advice.

You sometimes hear that the radio has taken over the political influence once wielded by the press; but there is no real evidence that this is true, or that in 1936 it brought about the result described. The radio is controlled by the same group in the community which controls the press and indeed, many important newspapers and radio stations are under common ownership. If it leaned either way, it would be toward the Republicans. But the radio, which is under federal license, takes pains to be as neutral as possible in political matters; it never takes an editorial position as does the press.

While the newspapers are conservative—far more conservative than the country itself—many people have a mistaken notion about the origin and extent of this conservatism. They imagine that "the advertiser" is the sole cause of the ills of the press, that the editors and publishers would like to be liberal and honest, but that the advertisers force them to be conservative and dishonest. This picture of firm blacks and whites is far from being accurate. While it is true that now and then one advertiser may exert improper influence on one newspaper, these occasions are much more rare than is commonly supposed. Local department store advertising is very important to most newspapers, but the owner of such a store only occasionally tries to influence the newspaper. When he does it is usually to get an elevator accident in his establishment suppressed, to obtain publicity for the annual outing of his employees, or something roughly comparable. More serious are the occasions on which, in the past, electric utilities have refused to advertise except in papers which were opposed to public ownership, or in which banks and other financial advertisers have boycotted papers with a pro-labor tendency. But even these are not the most important or the most typical situations.

The situation is that the conservatives usually do not have to bring any pressure to bear on the publisher, because he is just as conservative as they are and for the same reasons—personality, upbringing, wealth, and self-interest. In any community, the typical publisher is likely to be a member of the richest country club, and to mingle on even terms with men of wealth and power. Most successful newspapers nowadays are extremely valuable and prosperous. It is unlikely that any bank holds a mortgage on such a paper, and can crack the whip. I should be greatly surprised to learn that there are any papers actually owned or controlled by such groups as the National Association of Manufacturers or the Chamber of Commerce of the United States.

It is true that the editors are sometimes more liberal, more conscientious, more aware of their responsibility to the public, than are the publishers whom they serve. But even here, the situation is not as acute as many people innocently believe. There are plenty of working newspapermen who are themselves just as conservative as their publishers. Oddly enough, there are plenty of others who are without any political convictions of any kind, and who cheerfully take, without troubling themselves, whatever attitude they are told to—true mercenaries of the typewriter. By a sort of spiritual osmosis, many newspaper men gravitate toward papers with which they are in sympathy, wherever this is possible. In many cities of course, it is not, since the papers are all of one hue.

You can sum up the indictment of the press by saying that in general, it shares the evils of all capitalist society. In every such society there is a great suppressed debate going on, a debate, roughly speaking, between the haves and the havenots. The havenots think something ought to be changed and the haves believe that everything is all right. That debate runs through the whole fabric of our civilization. It bursts out in all sorts of unexpected places, and so does the pressure to keep it smothered. That is one reason why the attitude of the press is so essentially nostalgic, backward looking. It resists not merely the pressure of the future, but even the facts about the present, because it fears, quite correctly, that the trend is toward equalitarianism, and that is anathema to the publishers as it is to all other wealthy men. You are seeing it now in the discussion of the new British plan for a compensatory economy put out under the name of Lord Woolton. This plan, sponsored by the Tory government of Great Britain, is nevertheless too radical for the American press, which has refused to report it adequately, and has misrepresented and denounced it editorially.

In fairness we must admit that censorship by the publisher and by the forces of power and wealth is not the only censorship exerted on the press. There is also that of the audience, which votes every day for one kind of paper and against another, when it decides which paper it will read. Most people like to hear only opinions with which they know in advance that they agree. This may be deplorable; but it is very human. Every editor builds up an audience for himself consisting mainly of people who know in advance that they agree with his views. Any sudden change in those views would probably cost him the greater part of his audience, and very likely, his editorial chair as well. (To be sure, there are some cities as mentioned above, where all the press is uniformly conservative, and a progressive-minded person has to read a conservative paper or go without any news—except what he can get from the highly unsatisfactory medium of the radio.)

Where do we go from here? What steps are possible to make the press more responsive to the demands of democracy? Certainly there is no easy and simple answer to this question. We are moving in this country toward a mixed economy of private and public enterprise, and it is my guess that the press, which always reflects the dominant elements of economic power, will very likely move in the same direction, with increasing recognition of the press's public obligation as opposed to the private job of making money and trying to create or preserve a world in the image of its owner.

Actually, in some ways the press has been getting better for several decades. The average newspaper worker has higher educational qualifications than used to be the case. There are more experts on all sorts of subjects, and their standards of accuracy are higher. The Newspaper Guild has helped to bring needed backbone to the editorial worker, who now feels he has some weight behind him when he refuses to do a dishonorable act at the request of the publisher. Criticisms like those of Upton Sinclair have really had their effect on the morals of the press, though it would be asking too much of human nature for the publishers to admit it. A case in point is the *New York Times* and Russia. For several years prior to 1920, the *Times'* news out of Russia was appallingly inaccurate, prejudiced, and sensational. Then *The New Republic* published a special supplement proving how bad the *Times* reporting was. The *Times* promptly reformed, sent Walter Duranty to Moscow, and during the next ten years gave him carte blanche, with the result that his reporting of the Russian scene is one of the landmarks of modern journalism. It is amusing to recall that the two authors of *The New Republic* supplement were Walter Lippmann, now columnist for the conservative *New York Herald Tribune,* and Charles Merz, now editor-in-chief of the *New York Times.*

There is an important clue in what I have just said, for readers of newspapers everywhere. Editors and publishers are far more responsive to public pressure than you might suppose; after all, if they lose their audience, they have lost everything. Letters of protest to an editor or publisher, if several come at a time, and are not the work of obvious cranks, have a great effect. Clubs and associations could do much by appointing a committee on the press and sending the committee to meet the editor face to face and to protest from time to time, if they think he is betraying the public interest. In particular, as I have already suggested, every individual can help if he will subscribe to and read the best available paper, instead of the worst available one, which frequently has a circulation larger than that of all the good papers combined.. I should be sorry if what I have said should lead anyone to think I am complacent about the press, for I am not. As things were going at the middle of 1944, I can see only a slight hope of preventing a third world war and, before that, of preventing deep depression within this country. It seems to me that both externally and internally we are confronted by the necessity of making sudden and extreme alterations in our civilization, more sudden and extreme than have ever been witnessed in any country except one which, by complete bankruptcy and chaos, was inviting revolution. I see no hope at all of bringing about these changes without a great improvement in public opinion; that public opinion in turn depends upon the cooperation of the press, and we are not getting it. If there was ever a time when the collective intelligence and good will of American progressives should be called into action, it is now.

III: PROBLEMS OF THE RADIO
Bernard B. Smith

I T IS OF VAST IMPORTANCE in a discussion of the ways and means by which radio broadcasting may serve as a medium of free communication and preservation of the democratic faith within the American system of free enterprise, to recognize that radio broadcasting, unlike other means of popular communication such as the newspaper and motion picture, cannot exist except by express license of the Government of the United States. The ether—the vast, new, and mysterious domain unknown to the earth-bound peoples of earlier centuries—this ether through which the broadcasting signal moves from the transmitter to the radio set in your living room, belongs in established right to the people of the United States. The privilege, therefore, to use our air waves consists of a temporary and revocable grant issued in the name of the Government of the United States by the Executive Division of that Government.

Acquisition by the people of a huge portion of the global ether is one of the great and fortunate accidents of modern economic history. Every one can recall the jungle days of radio before the first law licensing stations was enacted in 1927, when frequencies and broadcast signals overlapped, and when the power of a specific station depended only upon the will of the owner of that station. During that period there was insufferable chaos in the ether without regard or hindrance from any quarter. A horde of prospectors were crowding into the radio Klondike, invading radio bands already staked out in the spectrum, drowning out weaker signals with stepped-up kilowatts, until the whole field of radio approached a state of sheer physical breakdown. The responsible elements of the radio industry then moved in on Washington, imploring Congress to establish control over radio broadcasting so that frequencies for radio broadcasting could be allotted in such fashion that no broadcast from any one station would interfere with the broadcast of another.

Acting upon the demands of the radio industry, the FRC was established by Congressional Act in 1927. This Commission, which was the predecessor of the present Federal Communications Commission, was vested by statute with the power of assigning definite frequencies to radio station operators in their respective broadcast areas and to determine precisely the amount of power which every radio station would be permitted to employ. In the granting of these licenses to operate radio stations a condition was imposed upon the licensee that he operate his radio station in the public interest, convenience, and necessity of the people of the United States. The right, therefore, to use air waves of the United States is derived from a license stemming directly from the people.

The fact that radio broadcasting depends for its existence upon the will of the Government is what distinguishes it from other means of communication. The broadcasting station, outside of its equipment, owns nothing that the Government cannot take from it through the simple process of abrogating its license. The station's right to broadcast is, therefore, anchored in nothing more than thin air, for theoretically at least it is permitted to operate its station only so long as it continues to serve the public interest, convenience, and necessity of the people of the United States. It would, therefore, appear that freedom of communication ought to be much more readily capable of being achieved in the field of radio broadcasting than in any other means of communication.

However, without launching into any academic discussion of the meaning of "air freedom" it will, I believe, be made perfectly clear that complete freedom in the generic sense of that word can never be achieved in radio broadcasting. All that we can hope for is to stake out a limited area within which radio broadcasting can serve as a medium for freedom of expression, for the enlightenment and for the education of the American people. Today, unfortunately, freedom of speech in radio broadcasting means in effect the right of the holder of a license to use the people's air waves to restrain free speech, to channel it, to limit it, to offer it to those who can pay for it, and to deny it to those who cannot.

It is true that the radio industry provides in the course of an evening, in capsule form, comparatively frequent short announcements of headline news, which doubtless provides some measure of information. But if the broadcasting industry were effectively carrying out the public trust implicit in the plain meaning of the words, "public interest, convenience and necessity," we would not find that 79 percent of the people of the United States do not know what a price subsidy is; that less than a third of our people know how a peace treaty is approved; that 60 percent of the people have either not heard, or not read, about the Atlantic Charter; that 63 percent of the people do not know that we are receiving reverse Lend-lease from Great Britain. These findings are contained in a report published recently in the *New York Times* by Hadley Cantril, Director of Public Opinion Research of Princeton University.

If radio were meeting its responsibilities to operate its facilities *in the public interest, convenience, and necessity* of the people, I do not believe that this deplorable and, what may prove tragic, ignorance on the part of the people of this country would be so evident.

The difficulty is that, despite the public trust under which radio stations operate, neither they nor the networks through whom they receive their principal programs exercise any reasonable measure of control over the programs broadcast over their facilities during the principal hours of the day and evening. For the test of whether a radio program shall be presented over a network lies not in the network's opinion of the public interest, convenience, or necessity of that program, but solely in the opinion of the radio department of an advertising agency. It is this agency, working solely in the interests of the national advertiser it represents, which normally determines the desirability of a given program—and this, in terms principally of the size of the audience the program is calculated to attract, for whom can be presented the glittering inducements for purchasing the particular laxative, dentifrice, or breakfast food produced by its client. The sole control that the network assumes over the commercial program is to assure itself that the half-hour offering does not violate any law, that it is not obscene or profane, and that it does not offend sizeable groups of the listening audience. The only programs over which the network exercises any true degree of control are its sustaining or unsponsored programs.

Manifestly, the national advertiser, like his advertising agency, is principally concerned with the size of the listening audience, and except occasionally when he may be interested in propagandizing or in otherwise doing a public relations service for himself, he chooses only programs that will entice and entertain as large a segment of the available listening audience as possible. Thus, between the hours of 7:30 and 11:00 in the evening the principal networks rarely provide any programs of information, enlightenment, or social significance. Those hours are now virtually preempted by the advertisers of the United States. Yet it is during that 3½-hour span that most people are at home and in a position to do any sustained listening.

The impressive statistics which the principal networks publish on their programmatic contributions to education and culture become meaningless when we recognize that these contributions are rarely broadcast at times convenient to the radio-listening habits of the average citizen. In fine, the advertiser's desire to sell his products becomes the dominating influence in radio broadcasting in America. Our large corporations have been particularly conscious of the tremendous value of enjoying a franchise to the air time of the people. As a result, eleven national advertisers are responsible for over 50 percent of the income of the four national networks.

It is an interesting commentary on the commercialism of radio broadcasting that, although a network by its affiliation contract can virtually compel its affiliates to broadcast any commercial program of an advertiser with whom it contracts it cannot compel its affiliates to broadcast its sustaining public-interest programs. Recently DeWitt Wallace's *Reader's Digest* undertook the sponsorship of the "Town Meeting." By reason of this sponsorship, some fifty stations of the Blue Network that had heretofore refused to broadcast "Town Meeting" will now be obliged to broadcast this commendable program. Thus, it is only because DeWitt Wallace's *Reader's Digest* is prepared to pay $15,000 to $20,000 for each network broadcast to Town Hall and the Blue Network that this public service program will now reach an additional fifty cities heretofore deprived of the opportunity to listen to it.

What has occurred on the cultural front in radio has been taking place as well in an equally vital area—the health front. Today, because so many of our doctors are in uniform, there exists in many sections of the country perilously inadequate medical service. One of the results therefrom is a growing and dangerous recourse in many communities to a kind of empirical self-medication. Manifestly, providing health information simply, directly, and effectively would be at the moment a public service which the radio industry should promptly undertake. The Blue Network has one such program called the Baby Health Institute. This program is broadcast mornings and was originally sponsored by H. J. Heinz. It is, I am told, an excellent program which has received wide medical support, and, when commercially sponsored, was broadcast virtually over the entire Blue Network. H. J. Heinz, however, decided to cease sponsoring this program. No sooner was the sponsorship withdrawn, than the vast majority of the Blue stations quickly jettisoned the program, so that today only about 40 of the 190 stations of the Blue Network are taking this program as part of their sustaining service. The Blue Network, therefore, in order to continue a vital public service, is seeking to find a new commercial sponsor for the program, in which event, it may be possible for it to succeed once again in having its full network take the program. For neither under the existing FCC rules, nor under the affiliation contracts, is there any method whereby a network can prevail upon its affiliates to broadcast its public-interest sustaining programs. So, whether or not the households of America are going to get needed health advice in this critical period of doctor shortage will depend on the skillfulness of the Blue Network sales department in inducing a commercial firm to sponsor this program.

On no other network in the course of the evening does one find any sustaining medical program, presumably because none of the other networks is able to induce a sufficient number of affiliates to broadcast such a program. So that we now find that the radio industry's medical contribution consists almost exclusively of the advice contained in the commercials of the proprietary drug manufacturers on the use of their pills and nostrums.

The prevailing credo seems to be: Why assume an obligation to provide for the health of the nation's body and mind when in providing laughter and escape exclusively you give the people what they will take and so sell them goods. Entertainment indeed has become not only the basic fare of the radio, but virtually the system under which it operates. Thus radio has joined the motion picture, the newspaper, and the ubiquitous comic book to anaesthetize the mind of the American people, offering them nothing that can induce the kind of thinking which brought this great Republic into being.

It is extremely difficult to believe that freedom of speech in the use of this medium is invaded when it is mildly suggested that something of deeper significance be offered to the American people, since it will always be within their power to refrain from being moved to thought by nothing more complicated than the twist of a dial. If freedom of the air means anything, it is freedom to listen to a variety of all classes of program; it means freedom to even a minority of people to obtain information and enlightenment by radio during the only hours they are at home.

The radio industry may well claim that it is the newspapers as much as themselves which share the responsibility for the appalling ignorance on the issues of the day demonstrated by Mr. Cantril's report. With, of course, a number of notable exceptions, newspapers generally have become, like radio, a source of entertainment rather than a pillar of enlightenment and a source of opinion.

And the newspapers have not been oblivious to the threat of radio to their economic existence. Fully a third of our radio stations are owned by newspapers, and they, together with the networks, own most of the powerful radio stations in the United States.

For a time, the Federal Communications Commission held up the granting of any applications by newspapers to operate new radio stations or to acquire licenses from existing stations. It had been the opinion of many that radio broadcasting should serve as a competitive counterpoise to the newspaper in the dissemination of news and opinion, of information and thought. Just as railroads have been prescribed from controlling competitive means of transportation and just as air lines are now opposing any attempt on the part of railroads to engage in air transportation, so it had been hoped that radio could exist as an independent medium in the field of communicaton.

However, that fight has now been lost and the Federal Communcations Commission has ceased to withhold action on applications by newspapers for the ownership of radio stations. No sooner had this ban been lifted, than a number of prominent newspapers entered into negotiations for the purchase of well-established radio stations: the *Washington Post* reportedly offering half a million dollars for Station WINX; the *Philadelphia Bulletin* $600,000 for WPEN; Marshall Field, three-quarters of a million dollars for WJJD; the *New York Times,* over a million dollars for WQXR; with others eagerly following suit.

One can little blame the newspapers, in their desire to protect their vast investments, for entering the radio industry, for it competes for the same advertiser support upon which the newspapers' economic existence depends. How much stronger will be their interest in radio when the facsimile newspaper is developed to a point where a newspaper can be broadcast into our homes and when with the coming of television, department stores can exhibit their latest Paris creations draped on comely models moving on a television screen, and automobile companies can project their sleek roadsters moving swiftly in full color before the eyes of a radio audience. For the prospective competitive force of radio's bid for department store and automobile advertising is doubtless already causing profound concern in the minds of the operators of the great newspaper empires.

Regardless of who owns a radio station, the fact remains that in the people's right requiring licenses to broadcast in the public interest, convenience, and necessity, the power exists to insure that radio serves to provide, to some measurable degree, a means of free communication, a means of enlightenment and information, a means of assuring access to the air waves for the champions of all sizeable segments of the American people, a means of affording the people in every city, town, and hamlet freedom to listen to all levels of information and entertainment.

Technical advance in the radio art moves so swiftly that one must never attempt to legislate for a period moving into a radio future that is certainly not foreseeable. For we are on the threshold of great advances in the radio art. Frequency modulation will make possible the addition of more than

three thousand stations to the 940 that already exist and will render it possible to bring communication by radio to the remotest areas of the country.
But we must not think of frequency modulation, of facsimile broadcasting
and of television simply in terms of mechanical improvements which like
the electric refrigerator will bring new ease and comfort into our homes,
for these products of American inventive genius can become vital instruments for the free communication of ideas and information if we the people will only will it by requiring our Congress to define adequately the
conditions under which the operators of these instruments are to be permitted to use our air waves. Facsimile broadcasting which is a method of
broadcasting a printed page with pictures and text so that they can be
reproduced cheaply on every radio set will make possible the establishment
of a newspaper in every home in the country. Who is going to operate
these home newspapers? Will they bring us a free press in the tradition of
the founding fathers or will they simply bring the comic book into the
home? Will television bring in sight and sound enlightenment and understanding of our great democracy into our living rooms, or will it simply
supply us with a poor replica of the movies to which perhaps a singing and
tap dancing commercial will be added?

It is not that I believe that radio should cease to serve as a medium for
the sale of laxatives, cigarettes, and breakfast foods. On the contrary, I believe that advertiser sponsored programs should be continued and employed to support other programs that are beamed to the public interest
and the public necessity in keeping with the plain intention and philosophy of our radio law. I believe that every network and all radio stations
in the United States ought to be required to devote during each evening
one half-hour to the broadcast of a sustaining non-commercial radio program. If each of the four networks would provide such a half hour, we
would have two hours of network time dedicated each evening, seven days
a week, to the public interest. This one half-hour would be employed for
free communication, giving access to the people's airwaves to leaders of
thought and opinion in America, to discussion and debate on controversial
subjects, to lectures on cultural topics, in short, to all fields of inquiry that
touch upon the maintenance of the democratic faith and the heightening,
rather than the freezing of the intellectual level of the people of the United
States.

We should not deprecate the support now given broadcasting by the national advertisers. We ought, rather, to take full advantage of the vast audiences they create with their intensely entertaining programs as audiences to
which can be beamed programs that are directed in the public interest. For
example, the Chicago Round Table is today broadcast over an average of

less than 40 percent of the affiliated stations of the Red Network at 1:30 in the afternoon on Sunday. If that program were broadcast between the hours of 7:30 and 8:00 on Sunday evening over the entire National Broadcasting Company Red Network of 145 stations, that program would be heard by an audience several thousand times greater than the audience it now reaches.

But here a difficulty exists—for as has been pointed out although networks can require their affiliate stations to broadcast commercially sponsored programs, they cannot compel them to broadcast sustaining programs which the networks provide in the public interest. After all, if "public interest" means anything, then affiliate radio stations should be required to devote one half-hour of their network time to the broadcast of a sustaining program that is directly beamed to the public weal and welfare. Mr. Paley, President of the Columbia Broadcasting System, in testifying before the Interstate Commerce Commission a few years ago, said that without network programs, network affiliate stations would lose half of their income. Moreover, it should not be forgotten that radio station operators pay nothing to the United States Government for their license to broadcast other than their promise to provide broadcasting services in "the public interest, convenience and necessity." Certainly, it is not too much to ask these licensees to devote one-seventh of their evening air time to the service of the people from whom they initially acquired their *lex operandi*.

We shall succeed in inducing the radio stations and the networks to surrender one half-hour each evening of profitable air time to the public interest only when educators and liberal-minded leaders in America become articulate in their demands upon our Congress. For the Federal Communications Commission, despite its having a courageous Chairman, simply is not strong enough, without something more than the tacit approval of educators and liberals, to stem the tide of commercial opportunism in the use of the air waves of the people of the United States. And competitively, it is impossible to induce one network and one station to adopt a policy of true public interest unless all other networks and all other stations are obliged to adopt a similar policy. Our only hope is to have liberal and progressive influence felt in Congress, so that radio broadcasting is operated under regulations sufficient to insure that the interest and convenience and necessity of the public, rather than that of the broadcaster, shall be the paramount objective in what is transmitted over the people's air waves.

Some time ago there appeared in Mr. Bliven's *New Republic* an article in which Senator Wheeler's status as a liberal was seriously questioned. I should like to remind Mr. Bliven that in the field of radio communications Senator Wheeler as Chairman of the Interstate Commerce Committee of the Senate has done more than all the liberals of the United States in preserving the people's stake in radio broadcasting. And he has steadfastly withstood all reactionary pressure in championing the cause of that stouthearted Roosevelt appointee to the Chairmanship of the FCC, James L. Fly, in Mr. Fly's efforts to preserve the interests of the people of the United States in their airwaves.

Those who are interested in attaining any measurable degree of free communication on the air cannot afford to remain silent. Unless they use the weight of their authority and the influence of their knowledge to bear upon our Government, it is unlikely that either the executive or legislative branches of our Government will attempt to lay down programmatic standards calculated to insure the freest type of communication consonant with a system of private ownership.

It would appear that there are two courses of action that may be taken: either to call upon the Federal Communications Commission to amend their network rules so that radio stations will be required to set aside one-seventh of their best evening hours in "the public interest, convenience, and necessity"; or, alternatively, to appeal to Congress to enact a law under which networks would be licensed.

With regard to the first of these alternatives, it should be borne in mind that the FCC does not directly regulate network or chain broadcasting; no authority therefor exists under the present radio law. But the FCC has undisputed authority (as approved by the Supreme Court of the United States) to control the conditions under which an individual station may broadcast network programs. Accordingly, educators and liberals should call upon the FCC to add a provision to the existing network rules to the effect that all licensees of standard broadcast stations who option any of their evening hours to networks for the broadcast of commercially sponsored programs, must agree to broadcast or rebroadcast each evening of the week between 7:30 and 11 P.M., a half-hour sustaining, non-commercial program, to be provided by the network with which they are affiliated.

The other recourse is to call upon Congress to enact a law under which networks would be directly licensed by the Government. Under such a law the number of networks would be limited. Provision could be made proscribing newspaper ownership of networks. This should not prove difficult for networks, as distinguished from individual stations, are not now controlled by newspapers. Such a law would provide for the establishment of programmatic standards for the networks not on a hit-or-miss basis, but on one that will provide for an enlarged concept of freedom of communication and will insure that an essential number of programs dedicated to the public interest are broadcast at times when people are home to listen and finally requiring every station on the networks to broadcast such programs.

Furthermore, to insure that no area of the country is without adequate network service, the networks once licensed can be required in the public interest, convenience, and necessity to devote a small portion of their profits to the extension of their service to those remote areas of the country which are without it, and which are not populous enough to support the advertising necessary for the maintenance of a local radio station. Precedent already exists in the operations of the Interstate Commerce Commission with respect to railroads. And networks protected by a quasi-proprietary status in which they are assured that additional networks will be enfranchised only as the economic and social need therefor is established and removed from the province of newspaper domination under a provision barring newspaper ownership of a network, could then set up rival news gathering organization vigorously competing with the traditional AP, UP, INS, and others in a program of competitive news gathering and dramatic spot coverage of important events throughout the United States and the rest of the world.

Our discussion here will not bring into being a law licensing networks with the concomitant benefits I have outlined. Nor can we hope that educators and liberals will compete with aggressive business entrepreneurs in seeking licenses for the operation of the great broadcasting miracles that will be the commonplaces of tomorrow. All that we can realistically hope for is to apply the powerful lever of liberal and progressive opinion in the halls of Congress to the end that the people's stake in this still new and illimitably expanding area of communication be permanently secured against uncontrolled commercial exploitation, and that the invisible electron in the unknowable ether be harnessed to a fuller realization of individual and social advancement.

4

SCIENCE AND THE
HUMANIZATION OF SOCIETY

I: INTRODUCTION
Gerald Wendt

I HAVE LIVED long enough to have seen a great change in the position of science in public esteem. There was a time when one hardly dared to mention that one was a scientist. But now every one seeks the advice of the scientist in one respect or another. The other day I checked the advertisements in one of our weekly magazines and found that 65 percent of the advertising used a scientific appeal, either displaying its science or pretending to, whereas only five percent of the editorial content of the same magazine had anything whatever to do with science.

Advertisers have been quick to learn that, at the moment at least, the country is interested in science and gives it rather superficial welcome. Because of the necessity for new weapons, because too of the necessity for advances in war medicine, there is at present a very much heightened interest in what science is doing. But it is not a real understanding. It is far from being what the scientist would want.

In some respects it is merely a childish curiosity about new and fascinating gadgets. Also, it represents businessmen's alertness and avidity for new sources of profit. But to a large extent I think this appreciation is false because it represents a worship of marvels and a hope of magic, a hope that from this miraculous world of science will come the answers that will never come by miracles or magic. Yet I think that there is in it one thing that is good: the public at large now admire the quality of mind that the scientist shows. I think they respect his integrity, and I think that they like best of all, perhaps, his optimism, the rather striking optimism of a scientist when he is faced with a problem.

In those rather elementary respects I think the present esteemed position of science is healthy, but there is much that is missing. For one thing, no one looks forward to the social consequences of these scientific gadgets. They do not realize that radar will completely revolutionize many of our habits in industry, at home, and in society. They do not foresee that an age of flight, of very rapid transportation, is not important merely because the planes will go so fast or so far, but is important chiefly because there will be so many planes, because each of us frequently, commonly, will be flying fast and far.

This is important if only because it is a tremendous new challenge to education. Parents ask me, "What shall we do about our boys and girls who will be able to fly off in the family helicopter for a week-end in Newfoundland, or a dinner party in Chicago?" I can console them only by pointing to the newspapers which list almost every day the achievements on the battlefront of boys of seventeen and eighteen, boys who normally would be babied by their mothers, but who now bear tremendous responsibilities such as I should shudder to assume and could not, boys who think not only well but quickly.

It is an education for responsibility that we need in an age of flight, but so far as I know, no one has thought ahead to that. No one has commented to me that television probably means a great interest in community life, in neighborhood life, in public living, and a great decrease in home life, because most television sets will not be in homes but in neighborhood gathering places, in the saloons and the bars, in dance and recreation halls. Indeed I hope they will be in every school and church too. This is the type of thinking that does not occur to people who welcome the oncoming of television.

So also there are those who think of the electric eye as a beautiful gadget. It is, but it will also bring an entirely new stage in the industrial revolution. The electric eye and the electric ear and various combinations of them make electric sense organs which are far more sensitive than the human senses and can duplicate every one of them except the sense of smell.

I cannot elaborate now, but I do say that if you read in the advertisements of the "automatic pilot" and the "invisible crew" that can carry a flying fortress across the sea with almost no attention, that can control the flight and action of a fortress from a remote plane or perhaps from a base beyond the horizon, then the *automatic factory* is not far behind. And that means a social revolution greater than the steam engine brought on us.

The social consequences of past science are small compared with the social consequences that are still to come from our laboratories. If this were the interest of those who now seem to worship science, I should be much pleased. It is not yet so. The public also does not yet understand what we mean by the scientific spirit, nor even by the general outlook of science. Men do not realize by any means that to us in science the great resource of the human race is nature. Edwin E. Slosson said it in another way: the great enemy of the human race is nature—not other men. The resources of nature have hardly been touched. They are ample to make a good world and a comfortable life for every one of the two billion human beings who are our brothers. But for that we must use our other great resource—the human brain. I am sure that there is hardly a scientist in the world who would not agree with me that with our resources in nature and in human intelligence, we can be sure of a better world some day. We can be certain we are not destined to misery and slavery. We can have our reward before we pass beyond this earth.

One other point I want to make: science is as yet an infant. What we have learned in the physical and chemical sciences, in mathematics and astronomy, is small compared with what we shall still learn in the biological sciences, and it is as nothing compared with what we shall learn some day in the more tenuous field of mental and spiritual phenomena, of telepathy, of means of direct communication between man and man, in the study of emotions, of feeling, perhaps even of a great cosmic consciousness, to use Ouspensky's word.

All that, too, will some day be the field of science, will be definite knowledge. It is because of that that we in science are both tremendously thrilled by what we have already learned and tremendously depressed by the fact that other people do not understand. Especially are we shocked to think that there are those who say that the end of all wisdom is in ancient books! That is the challenge.

II: THE SCIENTIFIC SPIRIT AND THE COMMON MAN

Floyd H. Allport

THE PURSUIT OF SCIENTIFIC METHOD manifests itself as a discipline second to none for the enrichment of life and the development of character. The change which comes over the young scholar when he gets down into the vitals of his problem is a striking phenomenon. The fussing, worrying, and uncertainties which he formerly exhibited begin to disappear. He develops an assurance, a poise, and a sense of working for something worthwhile, for something that transcends himself and all the pettiness of his immediate concerns. There is an exaltation of spirit which comes from forgetting one's self, and devoting one's energies to the disinterested pursuit of truth. There is no reason, however, to confine this observation to the graduate student or the professional scientist. If this is what science does for life, it will do it also, in some measure, at whatever level of advancement we take it. For it depends not upon knowledge or techniques mastered, but upon the expression of something which is present in almost every human being.

In addition to what it can do for the inner man, the scientific approach can also broaden the world view of the one who pursues it, no matter how humble or limited his pursuit may be. New perspectives can be gained upon the bewildering perplexities of the human scene. The scientific way is also the democratic way. Science and democracy cannot flourish without each other. Democracy requires a desire for justice, for an equal opportunity for all. But to understand the needs of all, and how in this complex world these needs can be served by working with and through one another, is a problem for the solution of which the scientific spirit and method are essential tools. Without them the most fairminded and democratic of intentions may go astray.

At this point, however, a basic confusion must be cleared up. Much of the modern stress upon science, in the layman's view, arises, I fear, from the remarkable advances in the inventions and processes which scientific discoveries have made possible in the last few decades. When we say that science has now become one of the most important phases of life, we are often likely to be referring to this technological advancement. But here we must be on our guard. The fact that we live in an age of rapidly developing applications of scientific findings does not guarantee that the scientific spirit will be automatically fostered in the thoughts and habits of citizens. The values which we are here considering do not lie in these end-products (or shall we call them by-products?) of the quest of science, but in the quest itself. Unless the citizen participates, even in humble degree, in this quest, or orients his thinking in the direction of this quest, the enrichment of living which comes from the scientific method and spirit will be lost to him. The fact that the technological devices which we use, and by which we are surrounded, are so complex that only the expert can see within them the workings of the laws of nature must act as a hindrance for those whose scientific expression must needs be limited to simpler things. Hence, the more rapidly these scientific applications advance, the further is the layman likely to be removed from an opportunity to realize the scientific spirit as a part of his own life. He can only remain on the side lines and cheer. Worse yet, he may develop a smugness and complacency, or an unwarranted and undisciplined sense of power, as he marshals the vast energies of nature by pressing a button.

Something far deeper than this is needed. We need less publicity with relation to the practical marvels of television, aviation, and the many other new devices which are going to remake our post-war world. Instead of all this we need a corrective, a note of true humility. We must foster the *understanding* of these devices and the thrill of the fumbling steps by which the basic scientific discoveries were made, until these latter become as vital an interest in the daily lives of citizens as the devices themselves. For the scientific spirit will give to human beings something which all the imposing products of scientific technology can never give, something without which their lives may become biased, thwarted, or arrogant, and their values insecure.

SINCE, THEN, IT IS THE METHOD OF SCIENCE, rather than its product, which here concerns us, let us turn at once to a consideration of what that method is. I would propose, as a working definition, these three criteria.

The *first* criterion is that, in his study, the investigator must deal, somewhere, or somehow, with the concrete, tangible, manipulative materials of nature. The things which he investigates must be, in other words, explicitly denotable. Though he may use abstractions in his thinking, he must never treat the abstractions as though they were the objects he is studying. He must never get too far away from his explicit materials; and he must deal with a sample of them which is numerically adequate for making his generalizations.

The *second* criterion is that the investigator shall proceed with the description of these materials and of how they act, by direct observation, and under the manipulative or observational controls through which their essential characteristics can be seen. Untenable theories are now discarded, and we try to formulate generalizations which will enable us to predict, even though imperfectly, the relationship of events among materials of the type which we are studying. These predictions should be later tested, with other explicitly denotable materials, by ourselves or other investigators.

Our *third* criterion relates back to the first two. Throughout the two preceding steps it is necessary to maintain a personal detachment from the problem we are studying. No ulterior interest of ours must be allowed to influence our observation or shape our conclusions; the phenomenon we are studying must be independent of our own wills. We must have as a motive for our study a curiosity to find out about things *just for the sake of finding out;* and this urge must be so compelling that it determines every step we take, every operation we perform, transcending every other value or consideration.

With this last criterion some may disagree. Some may think that the motive of aiding humanity, rather than disinterested curiosity, is the dominant and essential one in scientific method. Science for science's sake, they will say, is barren; we must have science for the sake of life. With this I cannot agree. I would reply that the love of truth and the zest for its discovery are an essential part of life itself. Hence, when we are pursuing science for its own sake, we *are* pursuing it for life's sake. As with any of life's fundamental values, we must lose ourselves in order to find ourselves. If we fail to do this, our endeavors at understanding our world will yield us little or nothing. Nature is an exacting mistress; we must give ourselves to it in complete self-effacement or we shall never learn its secrets. It is this third criterion, namely that of disinterested and selfless curiosity, which I would offer as the definition of the *scientific spirit*. One who truly possesses this spirit will pursue the method of science, and by it will guide his thinking and his conduct in every circumstance where it is possible or practicable for him to do so.

OUR PROBLEM now is to consider how these essential phases of the scientific method can receive a fuller expression in the daily lives of citizens. The problem is difficult because it deals not only with outer objects, but with the meaning of science itself in the inner life of the individual. It is complex because it is trammeled by every circumstance of the varied and bewildering society in which the individual lives.

As our first approach, I would offer the proposition that the basic meaning, the disinterested curiosity and spirit of science, since they are so intrinsically a part of the individual, cannot be given to him from the outside. This spirit can no more be directly inculcated than we can implant in an individual the appreciation of artistic or ethical values. If the zest for these adventures of the spirit is not already there as a part of the individual, there is nothing which educators can do to put it there. But it is my faith, supported by experience, that the spirit of the scientific quest *is* latent in nearly every man and woman. And here, as in all true education, the problem is not one of implanting something in the individual, but of giving an opportunity for the unfolding of that which he already possesses.

Environment is, of course, important, because the explicitly denotable objects which must start the seeker on his quest must be at hand. The access to these objects must be free, and their potential scientific interest to the individual must be easily manifest. But the clue with which we started will give us still another lead. If it is true that the scientific spirit is, to a degree, a natural part of every human life, manifesting itself whenever it is given favoring conditions, perhaps the best way to proceed is to take the obverse side and to examine the conditions of our society to see what *obstacles* may exist to the full realization of the scientific spirit of citizens. This approach, though seemingly negative, may turn out in the end to be the most constructive one.

THE ARTIFICIALITY of the surroundings of modern urban life are here a handicap more serious than we realize. What opportunity has a child or an adult, who has spent most of his life in an environment of subways, tall buildings, and elevators, to realize within himself the urge of curiosity about nature? The natural objects are already elaborated into complex materials and mechanisms for ulterior purposes; and the natural laws involved are hidden from view by the complexity of the device itself. A few years ago, before we were thrust into the hurly-burly of war, much was said about the gospel of leisure time and the possibility of a spiritual awakening through wise use of the free hours which our technology would provide. Was this really a justifiable hope? Far more than an empty gap of time in the twenty-four hours of the day must be provided before the ordinary citizen can turn, for the enrichment of life, to adventures of the scientific spirit. If we have solved for him all the material problems of his living by a few hours' labor in the day, if we have converted his surroundings from those of immediate nature to a world in which the forces of nature are already harnessed, the expression of his own scientific interest will indeed be difficult for him, and will seem unrelated to the rest of his existence.

I have no ready solution for these dilemmas. One can only say that we must work more aggressively to give citizens the opportunity for contact with simple natural materials. Demonstrations and exhibitions may help, always employing explicitly denotable objects. Approaches of a simplified laboratory character may be set up in adult education. More publicity can be given to communications of the Science News-Letter type; and the announcing or advertising of new inventions can be so presented as to share the emphasis between the utilitarian value of the product and information as to the basic experiments which made it possible.

An environment in which the materials for the scientific adventure are inadequate is not, however, the only obstacle which must be overcome. The psychological process itself by which the individual assimilates these materials, or tries to reconstruct them, must be considered. The problem of adequate sampling and of testing our generalizations is difficult. What the citizen relies upon is the all too facile use of oversimplified, and partially false, pictures which he carries around in his head. These stereotypes become pigeonholes into which the editor, journalist, reporter, and news-analyst file most of the communications which they receive; and these inadequate representations must serve in lieu of the objects and events themselves. Since these stereotyped impressions cannot be checked against the realities, the result is superficial, emotional, or wishful thinking upon a mass scale. News reporters and editors unfortunately do little to correct this condition; in fact, they often play upon it and make of it their stock in trade.

An understanding of this fact and its implications should show us the inadequacy of our present journalistic methods. Either our news-men must make an about-face and consciously strive to give the reader something which will bring him closer to the explicit materials which now lie beyond his ken, or else we must repudiate them as inadequate informants, and set up some new method of fact-reporting through which the scientific spirit of the citizens can operate.

Again, radio programs, even when the attempt is made to be informative, are made so short, through the fear that the public cannot stand more than a few minutes of enlightenment, that the speaker has to resort to stereotyping and over-simplification to cover his subject. In this modern age of quick summaries and outlines of "this" and "that," knowledge relating to the most abstruse subjects is presented in a nutshell, and often again by the use of stereotypes which defeat the scientific attitude of the reader. A similar charge may be made against the picture magazines. The interesting, often lurid, scenes which are presented incite emotions and encourage hasty generalizations without the slightest application of the logic of sampling of cases. Sometimes, indeed, the scenes themselves are posed so that they coincide with the reader's stereotypes. The experience given the beholder is thus vicarious, sensational, and distorted.

IF ONE WERE ASKED to name a condition of collective living which would be a first essential for the realization of the scientific spirit, one would have little hesitation in replying that there must be, first of all, complete freedom for investigation and thinking. The freedom must be not only overt, but psychological; the citizen must *feel* free to question and to examine every aspect of his experience. The average citizen, however, lives his entire life as a part of a great social structure. This structure is of tremendous importance to him, for it is the medium upon which he must depend for his entire existence. Whenever this structure is threatened, he must rise to its defense. This is true even though he may not be consciously aware of the grounds of his resistance. Now within this social structure there have been elaborated certain attitudes, feelings, and beliefs which are a part of its very being and which are functionally necessary to it. If these attitudes or beliefs are questioned, if they are laid open to investigation by the disinterested method of science, a vague, but none the less compelling, fear for the security of the structure arises.

THERE IS THUS AN INTERCONNECTION, immediate, or indirect, between every business production, exchange, and governmental cycle within the area of a country; and there is an interdependence between all these and the daily cycles and life-sustaining closures of the citizens. A *nation* thus consists of an aggregate of individuals who are acting for their means of livelihood and their security in one grand system of events, all dependent upon one another through a structure composed of cycles of behavior which are geared together and which cannot operate unless the other cycles also operate.

WITHIN THE INSTITUTIONAL STRUCTURES, or cycles, even of a small community there arise certain beliefs which are necessary for the continued operation of these cycles; and since these cycles give important closures to the individuals participating, the corresponding beliefs and attitudes are widely and tenaciously held, even at the cost of thwarting the scientific spirit of those who hold them. When we turn to the great society, may we not find the same principle at work? Are there not certain notions regarding the social order which it is necessary to believe in order to keep the wheels of our existing structure turning, and which are therefore axiomatically accepted, and are defended against questioning, by citizens and leaders alike?

We might find such a notion, for example, in the alleged right of free private enterprise. Employment, security, material progress, and an opportunity to acquire wealth and power are all closures which are made possible through the behavior-cycles of modern economic society. We want, therefore, not only to keep these cycles in operation but to expand their volume and to create many new ones geared in with the old. In order to do this, it seems necessary to us to hold the structure intact by keeping the events in the cycles which distribute the money counters about as they are. This means that the profit margin of counters can be kept in the hands of key persons in the cycle, and put back by them into the work of new cycle-elaboration and expansion, without too much restraint or diversion into the hands of those who function in the governmental cycles. The doctrine of free entrepreneural right is one preeminently fitted to serve this purpose. It establishes these practices upon the exalted plane of a natural right or law, and makes them immune to questioning. Through this elevation they are made to partake of the very character of our basic democratic freedoms. This doctrine, therefore, is widely accepted, and those who would critically examine it are frequently regarded as enemies of the social order.

Yet the doctrine of free private enterprise is in no sense a scientific concept. It is not a right founded upon natural law; and it does not stem from the data of explicit denotation. Indeed, when the social structure is seen not as a lone uncharted sea of enterprise, but as a closely knit structure of cycles in which the behavior of one individual materially affects the closures of all, the notion that it is the inalienable right of every man to secure whatever manipulative control he can within these cycles is seen as a baseless and dangerous assumption. In the very degree, therefore, in which this doctrine is employed as a support for the existing structure by shutting out the opportunity for raising questions about it, to that degree it becomes an obstacle to the scientific inquiry of citizens and to their attack by the scientific method upon the basic problems of their society.

Another notion which has been elaborated to serve the functioning of our collective structure is the doctrine of the corporation. This notion is arrived at by ignoring all the details of the cycles of human behavior making up a commercial or industrial business, and calling the whole thing a "corporate person." What this device has been able to do to oil the machinery of the economic structure is truly amazing. For fictitious persons can be endowed with rights and given freedom to function, and their responsibilities can be defined in whatever way we deem expedient. Through appropriate decisions in the connecting cycles of court action, opportunities are opened by this doctrine for the flow of money-counters, with a minimum of personal hazard, into the expansion of present production cycles and the elaboration of many new ones. Moreover, by thinking metaphorically of a business as a person, matters within that business can proceed with a simplicity which would be utterly impossible if we were to keep our attention upon the hundreds or thousands of separate men and women whose actions constitute the reality of that business. For the owner or executive in the system the corporate fiction is thus a device of the first importance. To submit the realities behind it to scientific scrutiny would be like questioning the very basis of his career. The worker himself must believe in it no less ardently. It is the ideology which makes the factory run. To be too curious about it would be to question the very bread which the members of his family eat. To our economists and political scientists, this doctrine is no less stock in trade. It enters vitally into their thinking, and appears upon the pages of their textbooks. The president of one of our great universities has called it one of the most important inventions ever made by man!

Yet when all is said and done, the corporate fiction is still a fiction. Notwithstanding the fact that it is an efficient device for the securing of practical objectives, it is extremely bad from the standpoint of science. In fact, a blind adherence to it makes true scientific method in the field of human relations impossible. It is not explicitly denotable, but only an abstraction. Useful, testable generalizations cannot be derived from its study. It ignores the test of disinterested scientific inquiry. Through its very nature, those who use it are those who have interested and ulterior motives from the start. Like all fictions elaborated to serve a given collective structure, this concept will work only so long as changing conditions do not require accompanying changes in the structure itself. When this necessity arises, its relativity and inadequacy become manifest. Though the corporate doctrine helps business to run and to expand, few persons would maintain that this running and expansion are free from accompanying problems, from upsets and dislocations of previous populations and modes of life, or from depressions, unemployment, booms, inflations, and many other frustrations and uncertainties.

The theory of the corporate person does not help us to solve problems such as these; it may, in fact, be one of the very reasons for their existence. If social scientists would begin to study society not merely as a set of economic indices, or as fictitious corporate persons and institutions endowed with inalienable rights and privileges, but as composed of cycles of the behavior of actual men and women interacting together and all dependent upon one another, important new perspectives on these very problems would be gained.

LET US EXAMINE still another example of our collective ideology. Not only the man on the street, but students in our schools and colleges are told that prices are regulated by the "laws of supply and demand." Theories are developed on this basis for explaining the problem of inflation to the man on the street. Bulletins and statements, circulated by our highest authorities, inform the citizen that the reason why prices tend to go up during a war period is that the supply of civilian consumer goods being low, consumers compete with one another for the purchase of available commodities; and this makes prices rise. This explanation, however, is contradicted by the most elementary objective observation. How many of us have ever seen purchasers standing at a counter and bidding against one another for the goods upon the merchant's shelf? Not many of us, I venture to say. To say that the effect is the same, so we might as well call it consumer competition, is, in my opinion, just plain self-deception. A much more plausible explanation, and one which is stated in terms of denotable human actions rather than economic abstractions, is as follows: A seller knows that the prospective purchaser before him has an unusually large amount of money in his pocket or shortly available. He therefore raises prices. He knows, of course, that the goods he sells are becoming scarce, and that since people generally desire or need them, a sufficient number of buyers will appear to take his stock at the higher price, even if this particular purchaser refuses to do so. There is no bidding of consumers against one another; because it is not necessary for the seller to make them bid. The price is not elastic during any one transaction. The seller himself simply sets the higher price, knowing that he will get it. It is, of course, true that someone in the wholesaling cycles before him has already raised the price, so the retailer has to raise his price also. Prices are raised *generally* throughout the cycles of the economic structure. *But make no mistake,* the principle is the same. Somebody, somewhere, *has* to raise the prices; they don't just raise themselves. They are not raised, moreover, in ordinary legitimate trans-actions, by consumer bidding, but by sellers' opportunity. The law of supply and demand, in a time of increased money circulation, is really a law of supply and *command.*

It is, of course, the duty of authorities to inform the people accurately and to encourage them to observe and to think clearly. Why then do they not give the people a more realistic statement about inflation? Why do they employ abstractions which, at the level of observation, become manifest fallacies?

No, the true reason for such teaching, as I see it, lies in the support which it gives to the collective structure we call our economic system. The ab-stract laws of economics and the metaphor of consumer competition are far more palatable than the implication of greed conveyed in the more straight-forward explanation. Were we to explain economic processes in this forth-right manner of natural science, doubts would be raised about the ultimate right of the entrepreneur to set his prices and to control the affairs of his business; and without this control we feel that the business structure may not be secure. Then too, the opportunity of expanding their business cycles, to which all sellers, or prospective sellers, hope to return in the normal post-war period, would be threatened. Higher prices, in normal times, will mean not only greater profits, but more business enter-prises and more employment. The corporate structure on which the worker and manager depend, and to whose acceleration they look for their increas-ing prosperity, requires the acceptance of beliefs which do not jeopardize its operation. At this point the venerable concepts of the classical economist come to our aid. The law of supply and demand and the theory of con-sumer competition will offer us a fitting explanation. All we need to do is to accept it, and to believe that it adequately covers the situation. This done, the abyss of truth can be safely skirted, and we will be able to carry on in our post-war structure as we have in the past.

But what has happened to the intellectual integrity of the citizen? He has now become a party to a set of illusions under whose spell the spirit of free inquiry becomes dormant and powerless. In so far as he believes the official explanation (and he feels it to be his duty to believe it), he will think and act as a loyal citizen should; he will believe that explanation of inflation which makes his institutions work. But he is doomed never to learn what inflation *really* is, or to what it is really due. Nor will he gain any realistic understanding of the collective structure to which his fortunes are committed and within which his thinking is controlled.

WHEN WE TURN from economic structure to cycles of political action, we are faced by the same condition. We might refer, for example, to the ideologies of political parties which mask the underlying realities of great struggle groups competing for the control of the behavior-cycles. We might check the doctrine that our government is representative, and that the will of the people (that is, of individual men and women) is being expressed, as against the closures which really operate in some of the political cycles. We might try to see what is concealed by the fiction of a transcendent Government which is alleged to be encroaching upon an entity known as Business. The time honored doctrine of States Rights is a similar obstacle to clear inquiry. The belief in the ultimate perfection of the Constitution, not to be modified except for the worse, is still another. Or again, we might weigh the belief in the automatic due process of the law, and the sanctity of courts, as against the events of court decision and precedent which have implemented our cycles from *caveat emptor* on down.

Public Opinion, itself, as an abstract entity, is a formidable obstacle to scientific inquiry when it is used as a symbol to bespeak support for practices in our political and economic structure; and this in spite of the real service which the opinion polls have rendered in clarifying this confusion. Public opinion of this sort is but the sounding board of collective interests and fictions. Our notion of democracy itself needs overhauling. We must be on our guard lest its freedoms be so distorted as to cover a set of doctrines which are dedicated not to individual liberty, but to the support and facilitation of our collective structures. The danger, in our modern world, of the loss of freedom of communication, yes—even of thinking, is a real one. Its source, however, does not lie, so much as is commonly supposed, in dictators, or in the control of a small and privileged class. It lies, rather, within the nature of our social organization itself, and in the controls exerted upon the citizens by the collective ideologies to which we are committed.

IF THE SCIENTIFIC SPIRIT of citizens is to help in the solution of human problems, most of us would agree that it must play its part in the ultimate elimination of war. But here again we find the same obstacles to its employment. We cannot think realistically about this problem because we have been unwilling or unable to see the nation as the inter-gearing of the behaviors of millions of men and women into a system through which their desires are satisfied. Just as in our internal economic cycles we have set up corporate fictions, so, in the national structure as a whole, we think in terms of a corporate national Being, possessed, in its own right, of principles, ideals, honor, sovereignty, and rights. This fiction, in its turn, obscures from us those real events through which wars actually come about, and protects the expanding nation-structure against a scrutiny or questioning which might confine its operation.

Our national behavior-system is but one among other powerful collective systems in the world. Though some of these—as allied nations—may gear together in a super-structure for mutual reinforcement, there is at present no one great structure, or society, which embraces all of them. Opposing one national or allied system is another national or allied system of comparable volume and power. Impingements of the two structures occur in relation to jurisdictional boundaries, foreign markets, colonial enterprise, and the use of the world's space and resources in expanding the economic cycles of the countries concerned. Warnings and mobilization then take place. Behavior cycles of military preparedness are elaborated in close inter-gearing with the economic cycles of each country. War, as well as the peace-time economy of the structure, becomes the *modus vivendi* of the citizens. Such structuring within a neighboring system produces a violent fear in the leaders and citizens of a country, for it threatens the very autonomy and security of their own nation-system; and in the sharp impingements of war which follow, there takes place a life-or-death struggle to smash the opposing system and to defend and preserve the national structure in which the citizens have invested their fortunes, their security, and their lives.

In such a crisis all the national ideologies are brought forth and exalted. The belief that the nation is a single entity flourishes as never before. The ideals which the nation is felt to espouse are heralded as the true issues behind the conflict. We are fighting for freedom, for Democracy, and for justice for all mankind. In the opposing system, also, the citizens are fighting for *their* functional ideologies, for the good of the State, the national culture, and other totalitarian symbols. The scientific spirit is at its lowest ebb.

I hope that my purpose in this analysis will not be misunderstood. I believe for the very reasons I am here outlining, that we must win this war if we are to preserve the autonomy of our national system, and therefore the security of our own lives. For this I am willing to make any sacrifice demanded, for I can do no other. Nor do I have anything but horror for the acts which our enemies, in the defense of their national structure and under the rationalization of their ideologies, have found themselves capable of committing. What I am here saying is that, regardless of the issues of the present conflict, we have not really understood what war is. One reason for this is that we have not understood what a nation is. And until we can lay aside our fictions of a sovereign national entity in our approach to these phenomena and learn to describe them disinterestedly, in terms of what explicit human beings are doing, we shall never, in my opinion, be able to understand them. Though this war must be won, the winning of it will, of itself, in no way guarantee a world from which warfare will be abolished. No organization of peace-loving nations can bring lasting peace to the world so long as nation-structures have within them the event-patterns and the ideologies from which wars themselves arise. We are dealing here with a problem which only the values of individual men and women, and the free expression of their scientific spirit, can solve.

THE FOSTERING of the scientific spirit and method in the daily lives of citizens is indeed a complex task. The obstacles which must be overcome, instead of centering merely in the ignorance, indifference, or emotionality of the citizens, lie largely in our necessary subservience to the structure and the ideological pattern of our society itself. A nation-structure is tending to become more and more like a machine. It is like a watch the action of whose parts must gear precisely together. The actions of the parts, for the national society, are the behaviors of the individuals; and these must be precisely fitted together—not only the individual's overt acts, but their words, their attitudes, and their very thoughts.

But here we meet a fundamental difficulty. For a social structure which is like a machine, in direct proportion to its increasing efficiency in supplying our creature wants, becomes more and more unfitted to the character of a human being. A mechanism, for example that of a watch, involves a pattern of events differing from that required for human living in two important respects. First, the purpose of the mechanism lies in the operation of its structure as a whole and what this structure can do to serve some ulterior objective. In a human society, however, the functioning of the parts must be for the benefit, not of the whole, or of someone outside the system who uses it, but of the parts themselves. The failure to recognize this truth is what underlies the monstrous character of totalitarian ideology.

Secondly, any machine, if it is to run smoothly and predictably, must. involve *all* of the actions of *each* of the parts. The parts cannot be free to deviate at odd moments, or to do other kinds of things upon their own initiative. What would happen to the watch if its wheels and pinions should suddenly decide that they would like to take time out and exercise the liberty to reflect, to realize their literary, artistic, or religious values, or to regard themselves and their neighbors as objects of scientific curiosity? And so it is with society. Although the actions and beliefs which are incorporated in the social structure can never be more than a limited segment of the individual's values and capacities, as that structure becomes more elaborate and efficient his daily living and thinking must be more and more restricted to these segmentalized routines. The values of art and religion, and of the spirit and method of science, since they demand complete individual freedom and guarantee nothing for the stability or operation of the collective cycles, must lie, if they are to receive expression, increasingly outside the orbit of that structure. This condition, however, cannot be encouraged or even permitted, for it may jeopardize the structure through raising questions about it, or about the ideology which is its support. Such a condition, as in the case of the watch, would violate the principle of total inclusion, upon which the continued operation of the structure itself depends. The only alternative, therefore, is that the pursuit of these irrelevant values be, in some manner (either overtly or indirectly), extinguished.

Yet it is in these very values, and the freedom to pursue them, that the hope of the future of mankind must lie. They hold within them the only possibility of our acting as whole individuals, as men and women who are free to bring to bear upon the pattern of their collective living the light of their own reason and conscience, and to shape this insensate pattern toward a better fulfillment of our human need. This is the impasse which we face. Our failure to surmount it, or even to understand it, is our human tragedy.

In all these problems we come back to education as our final hope. But it must be an education of a different and far more fundamental character than any we have thus far known. Education which merely trains for jobs, or which inculcates the traditional meaning of our institutions, our culture, and our social values will not help us. Indeed, it may lead us, as it has in the past, in the wrong direction. What we need, if we can find it, is the kind of education which will liberate the scientific spirit in men and women and establish it as one of the most cherished values of our living. It must be *self* education. It must begin with our scholars, our social scientists, our statesmen, and our public leaders; for the scientific spirit, like charity, must begin at home. After that, it will be free to extend outward, and to reach its full fruition in the common citizen. This new educational process will consist of the obtaining of insight, not only into ourselves, but into the very structure of the society through which we live. It will mean not only unselfishness and a willingness to relinquish many of our present collective interests, but also the use of scientific inquiry to learn what these interests are and how, often unconsciously, we are entrenching and expanding them within the structure of our collective living. Such self-education will require the humility and the intellectual honesty to abandon the answers we are now giving and the controls we now exert upon our thinking, and to go on without these, even in the face of a haunting sense of insecurity for the structures of which they have been the long-established support. It will mean, finally, that we have the courage to face the consequences of our own scientific curiosity, and to go forward to whatever changes our clearer vision may then require, even though these changes may be drastic and may carry us far into the unknown.

Men and women the world over have suffered almost beyond the point of endurance. No terrors of the unknown in our pattern of collective living could be greater than the agony of body and spirit which countless thousands have already undergone. Let us hope that this suffering will not have been in vain. Perhaps what we have endured, or may yet endure, will have been enough to start us onward toward the task ahead—toward the goal of a new insight whereby, though we cannot immediately solve our problems, we can begin to glimpse an understanding of their nature and to sense the direction in which their solution will ultimately lie. When that time comes, the world can at last be truly free. And one of the noblest of all the freedoms, that of a disinterested scientific spirit, can then become the heritage of man.

III: THE SOCIAL RESPONSIBILITIES OF SCIENTISTS

A. J. Carlson

MAY I BEGIN by making a comment on our general theme "The Scientific Spirit and Democratic Faith?" There is more to that phrase than the word "spirit" usually implies. I take it that we mean action in accordance with the method of science. I will not quarrel with words, but I feel sure that the scientist cannot have "faith" of any kind. My reason for that statement is this: if we know, we do not have faith; we have knowledge. If we do not know, we have no business to have "faith." If we do we are not scientists. We can have hopes, however, and I should like to phrase it as the Scientific Spirit and Democratic Hope, the hope that gradually, ultimately, the democratic processes of living together will work out; but as for "faith," I for one haven't any. However, I am quite sure that many of my colleagues in this group put into the word "faith" the very same thing that I put into the word "hope."

My discussion is to be, not the social implications of science but the social responsibility of scientists. Could we agree on this statement; The social responsibility of any individual or group *is commensurate with the understanding of such individuals or groups?* Not infrequently in this country of ours—and in other countries—the responsibilities of man to society are frequently measured by his political or economic position, by his wealth or his political power. In that sense, the scientists of the world are zero because they have little or no political power and they have very little cash—which I think is good for them. But pause and ponder my statement. Don't take my word for it! I am not hatching this proposition entirely out of thin air.

If the social responsibility of any individual or group is commensurate with the understanding of that individual or group, then the scientist's social responsibility becomes very great, because scientists should have greater understanding of the nature of man, the nature of man's environment, and the effect of the environment on man than have the rank and file of the population. If we have this greater understanding of man and of his environment, this imposes on us a greater social responsibility as to education and guidance of man in all matters dealing with individual, national, and international welfare. There can be no doubt about it, in my judgment, but don't take my judgment for it and don't blame the American Association for the Advancement of Science for any errors I may make. No one scientist in that great organization speaks for the Association unless the matter has been submitted to the Council of the Association for a vote.

Who are the scientists? On what basis can I say that a real scientist has greater understanding of the nature of man and the nature of man's environment than have the rank and file of society? Well, we think of scientists usually as those who have been trained in and have spent their lives in the physical or biological sciences, in teaching, in research, or in the practical application of the fundamental findings in science to industry or medicine. I would make the definition of a scientist a little broader. A historian, an economist, a so-called social scientist who really understands and really applies the scientific methods in his particular field could, I think, be included in the definition of a scientist. This is a matter largely for us of looking in the mirror, because it is perfectly clear to all who are somewhat informed about science in this and other lands, that all scientists do not have this wider understanding of the nature of man and the nature of man's environment. A person may apply his whole life to pure or abstract mathematics and never once get man and his environment practically into the focus of his intellect. An astronomer may spend his whole life with the galaxies or supergalaxies, with very little knowledge of this earth and its human life. In other words, even a scientist may be very narrow. I shall speak of that a little later. However, if a man is to be counted as a scientist at all, he should, of course, have the average modicum of liberal education, and if he is a scientist in one field, be it narrow or large, he will at least do this: If he does not know much about man or man's environment in the scientific sense, he will not shoot off his mouth or write a plethora of papers before stopping to find out. Unfortunately, so many so-called scientists are mere technicians who have not looked about and who understand as little of their fellowmen, the problems of life and the nature of environment, as do the most simpleminded peasants in the most backward countries in the world. So we cannot generalize.

My second point is this: *Science and the scientific method demand absolute intellectual integrity.* A person with absolute integrity is a rare man, a rare bird in this world of ours. Without such integrity science can neither persist nor make progress. In the nature of things, training in and serious pursuit of science, both in the fields of teaching and in the fields of research, ought to condition or train scientists to greater and greater intellectual integrity. Without intellectual integrity, particularly in social, economic, and political leadership, democracy cannot work—or, at least, it cannot work at its best. I think one of the serious diseases in democracy today—in other lands and ours—is the great lack of intellectual integrity in our leaders. How do we arrive at intellectual integrity? It is very hard to say, except by the trial and error method. In demonstrable fields, where findings can be checked and rechecked, we will be caught lying if we do not report our findings and our methods correctly. We hear often today that science, despite its great achievements for material welfare in war and peace, in life and death, has failed essentially to modify human conduct, and it has been asserted that man would be better off without modern science. Let us look about a minute. The religious mores, social mores, laws, rules—men have been subjected to these for a much longer time than to science. Science is essentially the product of the last three hundred years. Now, religion of the past and, to a certain extent, of the present, can appeal to two of man's strongest emotions in the way of modifying man's conduct. It can appeal to *fear* in the various tales that have been produced for our delectation, and it can appeal to *cupidity* and reward in the various "heavens" that have been projected. Essentially, that applies to all religions. But what have religions done to human conduct in these thousands of years? What has Christianity done toward changing human conduct in two thousand years? Well, look about you! There has been plenty of "hoc signo," there has been very little "vincimus."

Social mores attempt to modify man's behavior towards fair play and justice with the pressure of fear and punishment. We have oaths in court. Does anybody believe anybody else under oath in court or out of court? No! Now, all that science at its best can offer man is more and more accurate understanding.

My third point is this: *If men of science are to discharge their superior responsibilities to society, they must to their utmost ability step out of the ivory tower,*—I emphasize "ivory tower,"—and aid their fellowmen in the pursuit of and adherence to proven facts and reasonable inference through proven facts. The scientist must translate these methods, these facts, and these conclusions of science into the language of the common man. This can be done. I know there are those who differ with me on the next sentence but my experience tells me that the common man has the capacity to grasp science when so presented. I know there are many colleagues who say that the American college and the American university are wasting their effort on at least 50 percent of the students, or maybe more, who have not the brain to profit by liberal education. Well, I beg to differ. When rightly presented, practically every man, every young man and woman, can grasp the scientific method. The trouble is that we have so much poor teaching, so many poor teachers, in the sciences, even in the colleges, and the youngsters have been weaned away from hard work right through, from the kindergarten to the high school, and sometimes they get through some colleges without ever learning to work. Now, to me at least—and I think to other men—education is not play. It is hard labor with a joy all its own if you really achieve mastery, and most of our youth could achieve mastery so far as sheer mental ability is concerned, if they would or could be made to apply themselves.

I think that the common man has the capacity to grasp science when presented in clear simple language and it is of particular importance that all our fellow citizens understand thoroughly the method of science and the objectivity and the finality of scientific data. Without this, science frequently, in the mind of the common man, becomes associated with miracles. Without this understanding of the scientific method, the common man has little self-protection against current pseudo-science, quackery, fraud, and artistic lying that spout like mushrooms in August in the wake of or on the periphery of true scientific advance. I was a little disappointed in listening to the preceding papers on the press and the radio. Neither of the speakers touched on the tremendous amount of positive lying that is committed both by the radio and by the daily and the weekly press. By "positive lying" I mean saying something which you know is not so. Just a few illustrations: A generation ago, "Carter's Little Liver Pills," "Peruna," "Lydia Pinkham's Vegetable Compound," and "Duffy's Pure Malt Whiskey," did for human ailments what cigarettes and vitamin pills do for them in 1944. Someone from New York City sent me a whole page advertisement from one of the Sunday newspapers of the year 1900. "Four million cures, no failures!" Well, at any rate there was alcohol in the whiskey and there was some kind of cocktail in Peruna. Now, among these "four million cures" in 1900—not all of them in New York City, I presume— were 365,000 weak women (whatever that means) and about 100,000 weak men. Today, of course, we get what "pep" we need, greater vitality, etc. from cigarettes, vitamins, and what have you. Now both of these claims are lies, and yet they are printed and shouted in 1944.

There is no self-protection for the common man against this plain or artistic lying, unless he or she has sufficient comprehension of the scientific method to ask the advertiser to bring on his evidence. Contrary to the common notion that this is an age of science, it is an age of science only in the sense that *the scientific achievements of the few, especially in the way of consequent scientific gadgets and moderate control of natural forces have modified our material form of living.* It is an age of science in that sense alone. It is not an age of science in the sense of the common understanding of the scientific method and the integrity of scientific achievements. It is not an age of science—and this is most important—in the sense of less lying, deception, false propaganda, and the guidance of man by ancient taboos, superstitions, and false social traditions. It is not an age of science in that the scientific method or the training in science dominates or prevails in education from the kindergarten to the university. I had my eye opened on that point two years ago when, at the request of the North Central Association, I made a survey of the facilities and offerings in the natural sciences in some two hundred colleges and universities in sixteen Midwestern states. What did I find? I found that all the natural sciences combined, excluding mathematics, only represented 20 percent in the way of number of fulltime faculty and fulltime budgets for teaching purposes. Twenty percent! *But we could do marvels with that 20 percent if we really knew how to teach; in other words, if we had better teachers.*

There is absolute harmony between the scientific spirit and our fundamental democratic faith—as you have it—in the principles and processes of democracy. Both stress the responsibility and the freedom of the individual, a freedom compatible with men of intelligence and integrity living peaceably together in an increasingly crowded world. We hear so much—or, at least, I have heard for fifty years—about *states' rights*. I have heard so little about states' responsibilities, and that responsibility goes from the state to the county to the city and down to the individual citizen.

In my judgment, as I know biology, as I know the history of man, anything that decreases the responsibility of the individual is unbiological and will injure man in the long run. *Democracy does put responsibility on the individual.* All natural conditions which interfere with or minimize individual integrity and responsibility are equally injurious to the progress of science and to the progressive evolution and success of the democratic life.

However, this does not prevent the cooperation necessary in living together in peace. Indeed, such cooperation presumes an accurate and growing understanding of the nature of man and the nature of man's environment. As an illustration of this, let me cite the problem of health, food, and peace. In spite of and in the face of the growing world population, we more and more succeed in controlling epidemic and infectious disease. Science can increase the productivity of the soil for more and better food. It can aid man in decreasing the depletion of our soil in the interest of more and better food for more generations to come.

But human misery and human conflicts are still produced by overpopulation, and as yet, scientific understanding of man has not led to any general substitute for epidemics, infectious disease, starvation, and war in population control. If we breed like rabbits, ultimately we will probably have to live and die like rabbits. Some eight years ago I spent some months in Northern China, where the population even under normal conditions probably, or almost certainly, does not receive an adequate or optimum diet because of the excess population. I also found that so far as statistics show, one out of every two infants born in that 200,000,000 population, died in the first year of its life. This looks like a terrific biologic waste. But suppose modern medicine, prenatal and infant care, comes in and the infant mortality in the first year is reduced to something like what we have in civilized countries. What then? All you have is more mouths to feed in the land of the already starving. In merely stating this problem, science at once encounters formidable obstacles in the way of social, legal, and religious taboos. But even in this field scientists cannot shirk their social responsibilities. They must ascertain the facts. They must report these facts and endeavor to convince their fellowmen that we had better guide our lives in accordance with these demonstrated, rechecked, and inexorable facts.

Science, including the education in science of all 'men, concerns primarily that part of the human machinery called the cerebral cortex, especially the frontal lobes of the brain. According to the present evidence, the cerebral cortex is a much younger part of our body machinery than the top of the brain stem called the hypothalamus, a part of the human anatomy we have largely in common with all the vertebrates from the fishes upwards. It is this ancient structure, the hypothalamus, which so largely controls our emotions; that is, our animal love, greed, hate, and fear. The control of this ancient part of the brain by the cerebral cortex appears as yet to be both fragmentary and fragile.

Now, *education, including the education in science,* concerns itself with the cerebral cortex, but the primitive and powerful emotions of man—particularly greed, fear, and hate—frequently nullify the control of man's actions by understanding. Of all people, the men of science can perhaps best appreciate this fact, and the men of science should, therefore, show the greater patience and greater persistence in face of this difficulty. Greed and hate will at times prevail despite understanding to the contrary in every man, including the man of science. We men of science have the same hypothalamus as have other citizens. There is evidence, reliable biologic evidence, that the present humans on the earth are one species, but, especially in times of conflict, we do not act—or only a few of us act—as if this was a proven fact. In similar periods of stress, or, indeed, through propaganda of less respectful and wholesome character, we think that through extreme violence we will speedily produce a utopian world, forgetting that evolution of man in the way of control of his emotions by understanding is very slow indeed. Even my President Hutchins seems to think that we will reach Utopia by speeding towards a "new world" through education, but still carrying the same old hypothalamus!

Let me repeat: Obviously, our social responsibility cannot be discharged by staying in the ivory tower of science. Assuming that men of science are really educated, we should be on our guard against decreasing both the central and peripheral vision by mere attention to technology. I will be the last man to decry education offhand, or education through the hand. I was a farm lad until I was sixteen and I was a carpenter before I went to college, so I know what work with the hands is and I know the value that comes from it. But to spend 90 percent of a student's time in the so-called junior college, 90 percent of a student's time for two years in working with the foundry processes, cannot possibly give us a liberal education. Considerable could be done through better science education in the liberal arts colleges. But today the daily press, and the radio, touch more human minds, adult and children, more often and for a greater time than does our effort at education from the kindergarten to the university. What kind of education do we get through these agencies? Is it science? Is it integrity? Is it learning how to get at the facts and prove them? No! It is just the old drive of education by dictation that started 'way back in infancy and carried through the churches and through the grade school and the high school, and, I am sorry to say, frequently into the college. It is not a matter of *understanding* or mastery.

What, then, is education? What can we scientists do with men of wealth and big business who are able to put into man's mind that kind of shoddy junk via the radio and the press? That is a problem. The responsibility is clear. We are not all scientists all the time. There are too many of us in the ivory tower looking down on the common man. If we stay there for another three hundred years, there is not going to be much left either of science or of man.

5

DOES PROGRESSIVE EDUCATION EDUCATE?

LAWSON G. LOWREY, M.D., *Chairman.*

EDUARD C. LINDEMAN, *Professor of Social Philosophy, New York School of Social Work, Columbia University.*

MORRIS MEISTER, *Principal, Bronx High School of Science.*

JOHN G. PILLEY, *Chairman, Department of Education, Wellesley College.*

V. T. THAYER, *Educational Director, Ethical Culture Schools.*

Dr. Lowrey: After accepting the chairmanship of this group, I began wondering why a psychiatrist should be chosen. Then it occurred to me that people in my field have to do a great deal with children and their problems, and are constantly in touch with two things—the educational systems with which the children have to deal, and the fruits of the impingement of those educational systems upon the development of the individual child in terms of specific and general problems.

So I thought it might be well to have someone who viewed the matter from the angle of the child who finds himself involved in this or that kind of educational procedure without having any sort of choice himself as to what it is going to be or how it is going to work.

THE ARGUMENT

V. T. Thayer

IN FORMULATING OUR TOPIC, "Does progressive education contribute more than its rivals to the forwarding of the scientific spirit and the democratic faith," the committee planning this Conference recognized that conflicting philosophies of education are at bottom conflicting conceptions of the good life and differences in methods of education trace back ultimately to fundamental postulates of living.

Consider, for example, what seem to be the three most conspicuous contenders for our allegiance in education today: "Education for Freedom," "Education for Adjustment," "Progressive Education." In each instance the method advocated derives ultimately from basic assumptions regarding the nature of man and of learning and his relation to his universe.

Let us glance briefly at each of these theories.

"EDUCATION FOR FREEDOM" stresses the importance of a uniform curriculum for all students below the senior college in order to develop what is called their "common human nature" and it proposes as means to this end the use of materials that recapitulate roughly the cultural history of western civilization. The specific reforms this group would introduce into education are more clearly and consistently defined on the secondary and college levels than on the elementary, but at all stages of development the training of the intellect is the open-sesame to the education of "men as men." Take, for instance, Mark Van Doren, who seems at first reading the most sympathetic with progressive education on the elementary level. He begins with concessions to first-hand experience in elementary education. Text books, he observes, are "toneless teachers." The child "would rather hear, see, and handle for then he will remembr and inquire," and "is properly interested in the useful arts." But, even for Van Doren, the useful arts, as all first-hand experience, serve merely the function of a "kind of poetry." "The elementary pupil," he states, "as much as the liberal student, wants to do what he can do; and this is not to advance the world's knowledge. It is to catch up with as much of it as can be understood. The child, even more than the young man, is set for the permanent studies. His job is not to understand whatever world may flash by at the moment; it is to get himself ready for any human world at all."

Robert M. Hutchins is even more dogmatic. He sees only an injurious relationship between the maturation of a child through first-hand experience and the cultivation of the intellect. On the elementary level the prime duty of the school is to teach the verbal arts of communication. "Today as yesterday," he exclaims, "we may leave experience to other institutions and influences and emphasize in education the contribution that it is supremely fitted to make, the intellectual training of the young."

Only by means of the training of the intellect does it seem we can draw "out the elements of our common human nature."

Now most educators recognize the need for common, integrating experience that will unite students in certain basic ideas and ideals and develop common attitudes and dispositions. Particularly is this essential if a shared democratic culture is to evolve out of variegated racial and religious backgrounds of the peoples now composing our population. Indeed few will deny that an educational system, from elementary school through college and university, has already done much to create unity out of cultural diversity. Nevertheless any suggestion in these days of renewed tension that we educate for what is common to all men receives a sympathetic ear.

But let it be as well a critical ear! For by common human nature, Education for Freedom means a metaphysical essence in man quite different in substance and character from what we ordinarily conceive of as shared experiences or the social product of intimate association in common enterprises. Obviously an ideal such as respect for differences, the concept of the brotherhood of man with equal rights before the law, can originate out of and receive confirmation in a variety of experiences. For one a story or a poem, a historical incident or philosophical tract, will bring insight. Another will be touched more quickly and profoundly through the medium of the arts, a picture, sculptured figure, or music. Still a third responds more sensitively to the living touch that comes from working or playing with others in concrete situations. In each case, however, the recognition of the brotherhood of man and the vision of our common nature imply a quality of relationship with people, an interpenetration of life with life that men can and do in fact experience.

But this is not the common nature of Education for Freedom. Common nature as thus conceived is a substance or an essence in man, not a potential relationship or association.[1] It is a faculty of mind or reason containing within itself slumbering ideas or principles, that only one kind of subject matter or one intellectual discipline can awaken to action in an individual's life.

The concern to educate what is common in man prompts Education for Freedom to revive two assumptions of teaching in a form that it was thought scientists had refuted conclusively more than a generation ago. These assumptions are: (1) that values, ideas, and principles indispensable for an education reside in a specific subject matter, the trivium and quadrivium; and (2) that this subject matter, or discipline, possesses a magic

1. A careful reading of Hutchins leaves us somewhat confused as to what he really means by the fundamental ideas education is to convey. As major premises with which to solve problems of living they fortify his statement that "The notion of educating a man to live in any particular time or place, to adjust him to any particular environment, is therefore foreign to a true conception of education. Education implies teaching. Teaching implies knowledge. Knowledge is truth. The truth is everywhere the same."

On the other hand, the law of reason, the product of education "which is nothing but the idea of sufficiency," (*Education for Freedom*, p. 46), would appear to be an idea in the sense of an intellectual operation, a tool designed to harmonize the particularities of a situation with principles that do not need to be absolute.

virtue and can thus develop in students an intellectual power "capable of being applied in any field whatever."[2]

I hope enough has been said in this cursory summary of the fundamental principles of Education for Freedom to indicate its reactionary character. It is neither education for freedom, properly conceived, nor genuinely concerned with the scientific spirit and the democratic faith. It looks to the past not to the future for its sense of direction. The principles it would have men acquire do not follow from scientific investigation. They derive rather from authority before which empirical experience is asked to bow down. The scientific spirit, in contrast, insists upon inspecting the credentials of the principles by which men live and testing their appropriateness in terms of what they promise or effect in the quality and substance of men's lives. Nor do scientifically-minded people forget that the "faculty of reason," often in the past, has promulgated authoritative principles to justify human slavery, the bondage of women, the passive submission of subject peoples to an arbitrary ruler, and the subordination of children to the tyranny of parents. Indeed what pass unchallenged as principles of reason in one day not infrequently stand revealed later as prejudices, privileges, and long established customs; in short, as the products of a static society in a world that resists change. Accordingly, we are properly suspicious of a program for education that professes once again to reveal to the multitude through universal education the principles of our common human nature.

Nor is education for freedom consistent, as I see it, with the democratic faith, unless we are to interpret democracy in the individualistic terms of a bygone period. The democratic faith of today stresses the importance of people and increasingly a way of life in which the interests of one individual or group find expression through fruitful interrelationships with others. Thus are men challenged in our time to conceive of relations between people that are generous, not selfish, in their fundamental postulates; that stimulate men to contrive and to create ever enlarging circles of brotherhood in an interdependent world.

I find little support for this conception of democracy in Education for Freedom. It is rather an atavistic conception of freedom and the free man that characterizes the thinking of Hutchins, Barr, and Van Doren. The free man they visualize will doubtless be uneasy in a totalitarian state in so

2. Thus Stringfellow Barr writes in the *Magazine Digest* for November, 1943: "The man who has learned to practice these arts successfully can 'concentrate' on anything, can 'apply himself' to anything, can quickly learn any specialty, any profession, any business. That man can deliberate, can make practical decisions by other means than tossing a coin, can understand his failures, can recognize his obligations as well as his opportunities. He is, in short, what an earlier generation eloquently termed 'an educated man'."

far as he is disciplined to think for himself and to deduce his own conclusions from the truths furnished him by an individualistic tradition. But
neither is he a citizen of a democracy in which sensitive and responsive personalities seek to enter with sympathy and understanding into the lives of
others as a pre-condition of their own self-expression. On the contrary, the
ideal envisaged is that of a free individual, concerned, in Van Doren's
words, with "one's own excellence, the perfection of one's own intellectual
character." The mind trained in this school is in danger of becoming a
denatured reason, a reason which has successfully subordinated all pas-
sions and all human claims to its logical operations. Such an education may
produce the wise but disinterested individual envisaged by Spinoza who,
despite the evils that engulf men, "is scarcely at all disturbed in spirit"
but "always possesses true acquiescence of his spirit." It is less likely to develop the intelligent and generous men and women who seek earnestly the
brotherhood of man. I venture to suggest that the enthusiasm with which
this movement in American education is received by the crusaders of "free
enterprise" testifies to a nostalgic wish to escape the obligations of modern
life and to return to the free and uncontrolled social and economic order
of the past.

IN CONTRAST with the view that schools should concentrate primarily
upon intellectual training is that of "scientific education" or "Education
for Adjustment." This is specific and practical in its aims, dedicated to
"realism." It conceives of learning as habit-formation and quotes the be-
haviorists in psychology in its denial of originality in human beings.
Teaching is thus a matter of conditioning the student in school by means
of carefully controlled stimuli just as an animal is trained to predetermined
behavior by manipulating artificially the forces playing upon it. Indeed it
is from animal training on the one hand and job analysis of skilled operations on the other that this plan of education derives its principles of
learning and its materials and methods of instruction.

Do you ask for criteria to employ in the selection of the facts, the skills,
and the methods to use in education? Then are you referred to statistics or
to studies similar to those which now control the selection and use of materials and procedures of pre-service courses in schools and colleges. Similarly, it is held, values, desirable ways of living, of thinking, of believing,
are discoverable by statistics. Thus it is we can ascertain what properly to
teach in elementary arithmetic, the facts to include in a survey course in
college, or the indispensable skills of a vocational curriculum. Thus, too,
do we identify the subjects to eliminate from school and new courses to introduce. An inspection of the presence or absence of the material or the ac-

tivities in question within the accepted behavior of adults reveals its appropriateness for the indoctrination of young people. And since values and ideals, on this theory are reducible to the specific activities which identify them as such, education boils down to little more than the absorption of vast numbers of specific skills, abilities, and facts that men employ in the infinite number of concrete occasions of life. All the educator need do is make an inventory of these specific activities and to see that young people learn to perform them efficiently.[3]

In an extreme form, obviously, this theory not only lends itself to ridicule, it is impossible of application with young people. But in diluted form it has influenced both the organization of courses of study and methods of teaching on all levels—from arithmetic courses in the elementary school to survey courses in college. It explains the job-analysis approach to vocational education and the widespread use of study manuals in elementary and secondary schools that guide meticulously the learning operations of students. Its influence through the use of educational tests and measurements on behalf of uniformity in content and method of teaching is still strong.

Nevertheless, a year or two ago, many would have predicted that this overly simplified application of science to education was on the decline. Progressive education seemed to have elbowed it out of the elementary school and caused its influence to decline in secondary education. So, too, a more generalized type of vocational education was evidently replacing specific training in vocational schools. Thus Homer Rainey could recommend, on behalf of the American Youth Commission, that "high schools should concentrate their vocational training upon a program of generalized vocational education which would be applicable to a family of occupation. . . . Studies . . . reveal large possibilities of classification of jobs into closely related families in the sense that they require a similar type of training."

There is evidence, however, that the highly efficient and condensed type of training of students for specific functions in the Army and Navy is capturing once more the imagination of educators who easily confuse training and education. Already suggestions are emanating from influential quar-

3. As Franklin Bobbitt wrote some years ago: "The central theory is simple. Human life, however varied, consists in the performance of specific activities. Education that prepares for life is one that prepares definitely and adequately for these specific activities. However numerous and diverse they may be for any social class, they can be discovered. This requires only that one go out into the world of affairs and discover the particulars of which these affairs consist. These will show the abilities, attitudes, habits and appreciations and forms of knowledge that men need. These will be the objectives of the curriculum. . . . The curriculum will then be that series of experiences which children and youth must have by way of attaining these objectives."

ters that we reorganize education without delay in terms of what we have learned from instruction in the specialized training programs in the army and the navy.

It will be strange indeed if highly suggestive methods and devices do not emerge from these programs, but grave consequences may also follow unless significant differences between the developmental needs of children and young people and the specific conditions and requirements of military preparation are likewise borne in mind.

But our immediate question is the relation of this theory of education and training to the scientific spirit and the democratic faith.

I venture to suggest that it is neither scientific nor democratic.

It is out of harmony with the scientific spirit unless we identify the rule of thumb and dogmatic applications of a scientific hypothesis with the scientific mind. This school of education apparently derives its methods more from the psychological studies of animal behavior under artificial conditions of confinement than from developmental studies of children and adolescents.

So, too, it runs counter to our democratic faith. In its confessed attempt to train young people in vocational education solely for jobs now existing it may confirm trends toward the stratification of economic society that many students of society fear are already under way. Democracy requires a fluid society; one in which individuals are encouraged to find appropriate expression for uniqueness of talent and ability and to view both knowledge and institutions as open to change. Education for adjustment, in contrast, is education for the status quo, whether this status quo be vocational performance or the state of mind influenced by survey courses that convey only "the leading ideas and significant facts in the principal fields of knowledge" as determined by statistics. An education of this character looks neither to the past nor the future but to the perpetuation of things as they are.

I conclude that neither Education for Freedom nor Education for Adjustment is primarily concerned with the scientific spirit and the democratic faith. What then of Progressive Education? Does it, by the process of elimination, become the residuary legatee of educational virtues?

Not without qualification.

IN THE FIRST PLACE the term "progressive" is misleading. It is used not uncommonly to apply to practices and to conceptions of child life and of learning that are often as dogmatic and unscientific as those it condemns. Well might we exclaim in these days of slogans and stereotypes: "Oh, Progressive Education, what crimes are committed in thy name!"

Nevertheless for careful thinkers and earnest practitioners in education there is an orientation of mind, a sensitiveness to factors in growth and development, a way of conceiving both subject matter and method that contrast with the programs thus far discussed, and which we can characterize as Progressive Education.

What are some of the characteristics of this trend in education?

In the first place it belongs in the democratic tradition of the emancipation of individuals from class, status, and rigidly defined rôles. It recognizes children as persons, just as in the course of history women and slaves have in turn been encouraged to stand on their own feet and to go their own way as individual personalities.

Obviously the emergence of personalities out of a class group with predetermined rôles creates difficulty and confusion. When Negroes were slaves it was easy to decide how whites should treat Negroes, and Negroes, in turn, were said to know their place. Rights and duties were unambiguous; clearly defined by virtue of membership in the group as determined by nature and custom rather than by peculiarities of personality and character. So, too, with women before they acquired the rights of suffrage, equality with the husband in marriage relations, and some semblance of fair treatment in economic and civil society.

Now just as confusion followed the attempt to treat women and Negroes as persons as distinct from membership in a group with stereotyped obligations and privileges, so confusion has resulted from the effort to educate children as unique personalities. Quite naturally, in the early days of this revolution, attention centered too exclusively upon freeing the untapped resources of the personality of children from conventional inhibitions and suppressions and long-established procedures of a lock-step character. This was the era of revolt; often of sentimentality; of a new dogmatism. But for the past fifteen years at least (progressive educators have recognized) previous concentration upon the individual pupil, his nature and his interests, while all-important and never to be forgotten for a moment, was nevertheless in danger of becoming a one-sided reaction to an equally one-sided emphasis upon "the demands of society"; that it would defeat its own purposes unless the individual is envisaged as an integral phase of a larger dynamic context in which he functions as both the product and the creator of the forces playing upon him.

Accordingly, progressive teachers in recent years have had much less to say than twenty years ago about interests in the sense of inner urgings alone, and more regarding the needs of young people, by which is meant the context and the direction and the meaning of an interest in a social situation, as well as its private inner significance. This attention to the needs of children and young people requires professional understanding and, consequently, the progressive educator turns to experts in human de- velopment, to students of society and its institutions, to all who work and associate with young people outside as well as within the school, for assist- ance in determining how most wisely he can guide and direct the education of his students. The data derived from these varied sources—research bu- reaus, child guidance clinics, institutes on human development—now help to give character to the work of the progressive school. Teaching thus be- comes a profession since it strives to use science as one means of guiding young people wisely into democratic relations with their fellows and their society.

To the traditionalist and the intellectualist who know only one subject- matter and one method of learning, the verbal, this seems to neglect the training of the mind. Actually it vitalizes intellectual training by ground- ing it in different kinds of experience. For example, the progressive educa- tor emphasizes direct experience as one means of offsetting the limitations of an artificial and increasingly verbal civilization. He encourages second- ary schools and colleges as well as the elementary school to extend their interests beyond the classroom and the text book. He welcomes the tend- ency of colleges to use field work and work experience quite apart from its money return or its vocational implications (although these two have their place in education) in connection with subjects such as economics and sociology, and of secondary schools and colleges to provide service opportu- nities for students in agencies outside the school as one means of furthering social maturity as well as intellectual perception.

The progressive employs first-hand experience of students in order to give substance and qualities to the principles of knowledge he would have students acquire. But he is also interested in principles of conduct and in education for character. As John Dewey has said, democracy is a moral ideal. When the life of the school brings to expression through the actual participation of students the ideals we would have them live by, we may be certain it functions in moulding character; and this living matrix of rela- tionship constitutes the most effective medium for guiding students into wholesome associations with their fellows.

This method of influencing character and of introducing young people to the ideals of democratic living runs counter to the intellectualistic methods of Hutchins who brushes it aside with the observation, "since character is the result of choice, it is difficult to see how you can develop it unless you train the mind to make intelligent choices."

To which the progressive replies: True, but how do we best train the mind to make intelligent choices? By presenting it with verbal formulations or by helping young people through trial and error in the rough and tumble of their experience to sharpen observation and to refine judgment? Actually, of course, the progressive school uses first-hand experience and intellectual activity to reinforce each other. Experience that fails to eventuate in interpretation and is not deepened and enriched by reading is blind; but intellectual performance without taproots in life is equally futile.

I hope it is clear, from what has been said, that the progressive values as highly as the traditionalist the arts of communication, the use of conceptual thought, and the sharpening of the intellect, but he recognizes that these tools are poor tools indeed unless they serve the purposes of a psychologically mature person, one in whom emotional and social development have kept pace with the intellectual. He believes with James Marshall that "education should pay greater attention to basic psychological attitudes and drives. . . . The needs of a peaceful world and of a democratic and moral society—a happy land, if you will—require an educational system that will be conscious of psychological motivation and that will have the purpose of developing mature people with mature ends."

So, too, the progressive educator values the use of the past as well as the present in the education of young people. He recognizes that men are mutilated and helpless when cut off from their traditions. To know the nature of the problems that have dogged man's progress through the ages and the answers that the wisest and best representatives of our race have propounded to these problems, will equip us the better to confront the baffling issues of our day. We need history and philosophy in order to use wisely science and technology to improve human and humane relationships of living in a society knit sensitively together. But the knowledge thus acquired will be misdirected unless it enhances, not lessens, the integrity of our own lives and our sensitiveness to what is both actually and potentially novel and unique in our times. What Lawrence Frank remarks of Plato and Aristotle holds true of the wisest authors of the 100 great books, "The persistent perplexities and aspirations of human life that were familiar to them now confront us, and we must not evade our responsibilities by a nostalgic return to their formulations and procedures. As Santayana once remarked, 'a passion for the primitive is a sign of archaism in morals'; and, he might have added, a regression of intelligence."

Finally, the progressive school gives consideration to areas of experience that are either ignored or excluded by both Education for Freedom and Education for Adjustment. I refer, for example, to work experience not merely for its value in vocational guidance (important as this may be under certain circumstances) but more specifically for the purpose of maturing and stabilizing experience in social, civic, and political relationships.

Similarly the progressive school provides generous opportunities for aesthetic and artistic development not merely because of their indispensable contributions to personal growth but as one means of widening sympathy and enhancing the capacity to enter appreciatively into the lives of others —surely a prime essential for democratic relationships among people.

But, it is asked, what are the results of this progressive education? Does it not encourage inefficient and sloppy mental habits, superficial interests, an inability to size up a job and to see it through to completion?

Valid evidence of the results of one educational procedure, particularly a school experience, is of course difficult to secure in view of the many factors in life that make for success or failure, for a healthy or distorted personality. Nevertheless we do have available the conclusions of a thoroughgoing appraisal of the records of students who have entered colleges from the progressive schools in the Eight Year Experiment. This evidence indicates that students from progressive schools do slightly better academically than do conventionally educated students with similar economic, cultural, and racial backgrounds. When a generous sampling of progressive students was paired with students of like background who entered college from schools outside the experiment, it was found that the progressive group achieved grades of equal if not slightly better caliber than other students, but in addition they participated more than others in campus activities, were more concerned with contemporary affairs, engaged to the same extent in social life, and were more interested in aesthetic experiences, of both an appreciative and creative character.

It is thus fairly evident that progressive secondary schools at least do not prevent their students from succeeding in college as colleges are now constituted. This is gratifying but, of course, does not answer the main problem of education, which as I indicated earlier reduces to the question of life values. The chief contribution of progressive education consists in the fact that it seeks ever to adapt its practices to the needs of young people as these are revealed by scientific studies and to help young people to meet their needs in ways designed to further the democratic faith.

THE DISCUSSION

DR. LINDEMAN: As I understand Dr. Thayer's position, he insists that those of us who believe in progressive education shall begin the statement of our premise by stating that our primary interest is in human personality. He then goes on to say that personal growth takes place in a cultural environment and that this environment makes certain claims upon the person. If, for example, he lives and grows in a democratic society, this fact exists as a claim upon his learning. With all of this I thoroughly agree and also with his insistence that science and technology are significant environmental factors, that the continuity of the learner's cultural history exists as a claim, and finally that there are moral claims as well. The question I wish to ask arises from the fact that among the opponents of progressive education one now finds many religionists. Did Dr. Thayer purposely omit religion from his list of cultural elements? Or, stated otherwise, does Dr. Thayer believe that progressive educators should take account of the religious factor in our culture? It is my impression that the criticism of modern education which comes from both the high I. Q. and the low I. Q. religious groups is the most formidable attack we have to meet.

DR. THAYER: If you read Maritain, for example, and certain groups in the field of religion, you have a type of progressive education that gives place to interests and recognizes the importance of creative approach to life, and that it is a function of education to help people deal with their environment creatively. But it holds in reserve always ultimate conformity to certain dogmas. That is what you have in Maritain,—everything that you would ask for in the fostering of personality, including creativeness and originality, provided you come out in the right way as regards dogma at the end. That in turn takes us into the question of whether we are going to be satisfied to define the natural realm as these educators for adjustment tend to do, merely in mechanical terms, merely in terms (as Hutchins says) of the beast in us, or whether we recognize in the natural realm and in human beings all of these spiritual qualities that we value so highly, which are just as natural and just as original in human beings as the so-called beast in us, or the habitual actions, and the like.

I think eventually progressive education will have to resolve that difficulty. Different people will come out with different answers. But I include in character development, in the identification of young people with the ethical principles of democracy, the belief in the worth of the individual, respect for the integrity of the personality, and the development of one's own unique talents and abilities in such a way that in the process of self-expression one contributes to the life of those with whom one is identified.

I call these spiritual or religious values. Any school that concerns itself with character development is concerning itself with religious values.

DR. LOWREY: We tend unjustifiably to mix rituals, creeds, and forms of religious observance with the essential spiritual values of man. If there is anything which this country has tried to stand for, it has been the notion that there were spiritual values in and for all types of men, but that they were all free to choose the particular ritual or form they wanted to follow. Of course, that is true only within limits because we indoctrinate our children from a very early age.

Mr. Meister: There is a current of thought in Dr. Thayer's presentation which seems to set up some straw men and then knock them down. In offering apologies for the errors of the early progressive movement, he seems to be agreeing with some of the more acceptable aspects of the Hutchins philosophy and of the "education for adjustment" philosophy.

Thus, for example, when he resolves the conflict between interests and needs, he is borrowing in part from the other analyses. When he resolves the conflict between matter and method, between the individual and society, between the doctrines of discipline and freedom, and the extent to which there must be discipline in freedom, when he develops his concept of the common human nature which does exist or of the problem of transmitting the cultural heritage to the individual, or the controversy between general education and vocational education, in all these resolutions, it seems to me that there is indicated a fusion of the better elements in all three points of view analyzed in his paper.

But perhaps I do not fully understand Dr. Thayer's meaning. Let me therefore turn to other aspects with which I am somewhat more familiar. Obviously, unless a philosophy or a point of view finds its application in the trenches of educational work, in real classrooms, with real children in public school situations, then we have not gone very far. I happen to be working in a situation which had some advantages that other public schools do not have. With respect to a philosophy of education, the school has adopted science as the core of the curriculum. With regard to the student body, it has the advantage of segregating a group of better-than-average intelligence, so that the problem is not complicated by what so many of us in the public schools suffer from, the so-called low I.Q. or non-academically-minded child. We have a third advantage in that we have a group of parents who are intelligent, who recognize the value of education, and who cooperate with the school.

We also have the advantage of a faculty who are competent. They like and understand children. Most of them have children of their own. I think that this faculty, if one were to examine them individual by individual, would in the main be willing to cast his or her lot with the tenets of democratic faith that have been presented by Dr. Thayer.

Yet what do we find in such a group as this and in such a school as this with regard to practical implementation? We are plagued constantly by a number of difficulties, some of them almost impossible to overcome. We are plagued by the bigness of the system. We are plagued by a system and a method of accounting of manpower and of educational facilities which focuses upon such yardsticks as pupil-periods rather than individual needs.

We are plagued constantly by the limitations of such objective things as classrooms and space. Charts are drawn indicating how often in the day each room is used. We are plagued by large classes. We are plagued by a heavy teaching load. We are plagued, strangely enough, by the rigidity of teacher tenure. Very often the acceptance of the democratic faith and the scientific spirit becomes a vague and hardly discernible element in the life of the teacher. As a person only after school hours, a dualism is set up between his life with the children and his life as a thinking and creative human being.

We are all subject to the well-known law of inertia. The human flesh is often weak. It seems easier to proceed in a given direction or at a given pace because it requires a force to change that pace or to change that direction. For example, we tend to persist in the compartmentalization of knowledge, not realizing the contradiction involved in the acceptance of democracy and the implications of subject-matter compartmentalization. We tend to react against the heavy teaching load with a rigidity and a persistence for certain formulae; the very formulae that bigness and system foist upon us. Very often when, in attempting to meet the individual needs of children, we find ourselves departing from such formulae, as for instance twenty-five teaching periods per teacher per week, there is a hesitancy to depart from that formula that sometimes borders on revolt.

As a result, the very people who profess faith in democratic philosophy will neglect the needs of children hungry for laboratory experiences, for clubs, for forums, for social activities. Even listening to and educating the parents must sometimes be neglected because it takes somebody's time and goes beyond the formula that the system foists upon us. Problems in health education, too, are often ignored.

It would seem to me that the situation on the battlefield of democracy, on this front we are fighting on, calls for a spirit of altruism on the part of all workers. They must not wait until all of the problems are solved by directors of budgets and by administrators at the top. Teachers must have sufficient self-sacrifice in their nature to be willing to work with children regardless of what it entails in effort; because the consequences are serious. The people on the other side of the fence are much wiser than we. Having accepted a dogma or having adopted a faith, we do not talk so much about it. They attack the problem at the very core. They have learned how to take advantage of the bigness of our system and their program of action is exerting an increasingly powerful influence.

When educational workers, imbued with the democratic philosophy, align themselves with labor and unionism, they are doing a splendid thing, but in doing so they often make the mistake of slavishly imitating the methods, the practices, the program in toto of the economic struggle. Having aligned themselves with labor, many believe that it would show a false dignity if they called themselves, and sought to be, professionals as well.

We must, in our own lives as educational workers in public school systems, try to fuse, combine, and resolve the problem of being true professionals while siding with labor and all of the other liberal forces in society today.

DR. LOWREY: It so happens that I do know and have known over a long period of years a great many adolescents and children. And I found myself seriously disturbed when the generals in the Army were saying that our boys were uneducated, they couldn't do higher mathematics of one form or another, and they were soft. What really blew my top, to use a good slang expression, was Cal Tinney saying on the radio one night that "The American boys were soft; they couldn't climb trees."

Well, what that had to do with the problem of whether they could *learn* to climb trees, if they had to, I don't know. I became very indignant and said publicly that of course they are soft as far as mass murder is concerned, but that does not mean that they have not the capacity to learn and that they have not the background to learn all these things and to adapt to them. My personal experience is that those who come through a progressive educational type of training have a greater adaptability, a greater basic something that permits them to adjust themselves to all sorts of situations.

A short time ago I read what struck me as one of the finest definitions of democracy and democratic faith I have ever seen. It is quoted from a speech by Bernard Baruch at a dinner in his honor: "Some ask why we fight. This is my answer. We fight for ancient rights unnoticed as the breath we draw, leave to live by no man's leave underneath the law."

I wonder if that last sentence hasn't a lot to do with this democracy and democratic faith we are talking about.

DR. PILLEY: In this discussion we are attempting to judge a variety of educational policies by the extent to which they serve the democratic ideal. But so far we in our discussion have not paid much regard to the point Dr. Thayer made when he quoted Professor Dewey as saying that democracy is a moral ideal. Dr. Lindeman seemed to be coming close to this point when he asked what part religion should play in progressive education. Even so we have said very little about the extent to which the various educational policies outlined by Dr. Thayer are likely to contribute to the kind of moral development necessary for democracy.

I would like to say something about some common misunderstandings of moral education. Of these perhaps the commonest shows itself in the idea that moral education takes place of itself as young people learn to live a common way of life. The inadequacy of this view becomes apparent as soon as we remember that the Nazis have developed a common way of life. The kind of moral development upon which that rests is certainly of a very different kind from that we associate with democracy. But even those who insist that moral education depends upon the common life developed being a good common life may still not recognize what is essential in moral education. We sometimes hear teachers talking as though moral education consisted in young people's learning to understand and to conform with the ways of the society into which they were born. This view with its corollary that moral education is relative to the society in which it exists seems to me a thoroughly mistaken idea.

To my mind moral education consists in young people developing a vision of personal and social excellence, and making this vision the guiding principle in their lives. To develop such a vision of moral excellence, as in developing a vision of artistic excellence, they must learn to develop the sensibility upon which the discernment of excellence depends. To give it expression they must learn to understand themselves and, through it, the human consequences of their actions: they must then strive to act in ways which do most to realize their vision of excellence. Moral education in this sense does not necessarily lead people to approve of the ideals and of the ways of living that are generally accepted in the group to which they belong. It leads to their being able to compare what exists with their vision of excellence and, when necessary, to denounce it as bad, as did the prophets of old.

It is only when people are morally educated in this sense that they can be effective members of democracy. It is certainly only then that they can claim the title of progressive. Thus one of the democratic educator's main responsibilities is to help his pupils develop moral sensibility and power of discernment. In doing this he must respect every genuine feeling on their part including those in which he may feel they are seriously mistaken. He must remember that the future of the world is in the hands of those he teaches. If in the name of "guidance" he should concern himself with teaching his pupils merely to conform with the ways of living that happen to be current in his generation he will be destroying the imaginative freedom that must be theirs if they are to make a better world.

If we accept the view that it is only through moral education in this sense that democracy can be improved it is important to ask what importance is attached to it by the three educational movements Dr. Thayer outlined for us.

Beginning with Education for Freedom we recognize two things on the positive side. We see great importance being attached to young peoples' learning to appreciate human excellence as expressed in literary and scientific masterpieces. We also see great importance attached to their learning to exercise judgment. The value of these emphases to young people's moral development is however made very doubtful by the fact that the great books chosen for study are the expression of intellectual rather than of moral understanding and by the fact that the kind of judgment encouraged is mainly that called into play by interpreting difficult texts. By concentrating on the study of texts and by neglecting the all-important educational question of how life and letters may be made to bring illumination to one another Education for Freedom is much more likely to encourage students in verbalistic skills than in understanding themselves and their fellows. Its contribution to moral education may also be questioned on the ground that it shows no respect for students' particular interests and abilities. In this it provides the poorest example of moral behavior. Its contribution may be further questioned on the ground that it scorns the study of the world as it is; forgetting that without an understanding of the world as it is even the most nobly conceived ideal is not likely to make very effective headway.

Education for Adjustment, judged by its regard for the moral aspect of education makes very sorry showing indeed. It subscribes to the philosophy of Dr. Pangloss that "Everything is for the best in the best of all possible worlds" without any of his trials and adversities to justify so defeatist a conclusion. By asserting that human beings should adapt themselves to what exists it urges them to abandon the kind of thinking and the kind of endeavor upon which moral improvement depends. To call this education is to abuse the word.

Progressive Education when judged by its contribution to moral education makes a far better showing. Progressive Education is animated by the desire to bring about a greater development of human potentialities and with it a more real kind of democracy. It emphasizes the principle that human beings learn to do by doing and in this it recognizes also the importance of ensuring that life and letters be made to bring illumination to one another. Even so I feel that in describing their work, progressive educators do not as a rule give a sufficiently detailed account of how they conceive of the moral aspect of their task. Sometimes they even talk as though, by the proper use of scientific methods, moral issues could be avoided altogether.

I felt something of this even in Dr. Thayer's account of Progressive Education. I hoped that after describing the shortcomings of Education for Adjustment he would go on to say how in contrast with it, Progressive Education sought to encourage in students a sense of excellence which would enable them to make a better world. Instead he praised Progressive Education for basing its policies on the scientific study of children's "needs." In doing this he seemed to me to be leaving out of account the fact that the word "needs" makes no sense except in reference to some purpose or ideal for which the thing referred to is needed. It is only when there is agreement as to what the purpose is that there can be agreement as to what is "needed" for its attainment. In the case of such "needs" as those for food or clothing there is not likely to be much disagreement about the purpose. But when it comes to the "needs" upon which personal development depends disagreements may be considerable and difficult to reconcile. When there are disagreements about the ideals to be pursued there are necessarily also disagreements about "needs." Since Hitler's social ideals are different from ours we would hardly expect him to have the same conception of childrens "needs" as we do. But even when there is agreement as to children's needs it is important to be clear about the ideals which they further. Often the agreement reached between teachers as to children's needs depends on a commonly accepted but unexamined ideal of the kind suggested by such expressions as "a mature personality" or "wholesome relationship" or "worthwhile interests." If teachers accept such expressions as providing a sufficient definition of educational ideals it is not difficult for them to go on to assume that scientific studies can reveal what is "needed" for their attainment. This assumption is however ill-founded, for unless the ideal is clearly thought out and unless it is possible to recognize in practice what developments are leading towards its realization there is no means of telling whether anything regarded as a "need" is truly effective in furthering the ideal. In the meantime the assumption that "needs" can be scientifically ascertained carries with it a serious misunderstanding of the nature of scientific inquiry. Science, though it can tell us what is likely to result from any particular kind of treatment of children, cannot tell us which of a number of possible courses of action it is best to pursue. Thus however much progress is made in developing techniques of child study it in no way reduces the teacher's responsibility for developing a vision of moral excellence and for helping his pupils to do the same.

At places in Dr. Thayer's account of Progressive Education I felt he was on the threshold of discussing the encouragement of young people's moral understanding, yet on each occasion he fell back on expressions which seemed to me to avoid the issue. Having heard him say that scientific experts could tell us what childrens' "needs" were I began to be alarmed lest they should also be telling us what "wholesome relationships" or "mature personalities" are.

It would seem to me that the success of any educational policy in furthering the democratic cause depends upon the degree to which it shows an awareness of the importance of encouraging young people in the development of moral understanding. If it shows this only in a low degree, or if it assumes that moral education consists merely in young people's learning to conform with the demands made by society, it must inevitably encourage moral skepticism and with it, self-centredness. Amongst the young people I teach I find an alarmingly high proportion, even today, saying such things as "Who is to say that Hitler isn't right? He has his values and we have ours. They happen to be in conflict with ours, so we have to fight him. But that doesn't mean he is wrong." Such things are to my mind a clear sign of what has been lacking in traditional education.

It is, I know, the purpose of Progressive Education to restore the kind of moral consciousness which leads to a discernment of what is excellent and of what is base, but I feel it is a great pity that progressive educators do not make their thought on this aspect of the educational problem more clear. I felt that it was with this in mind that Dr. Lindeman asked about the contribution religious teaching could make to education. I do not know what he regards the relationship between religious and moral values to be, but I think I should say that in my view it is a serious misunderstanding of religion to regard religious values as separate from those that are expressed in the way you behave to your neighbor, in the way you love your friends, and in the way you serve your community.

DR. THAYER: I think I would say in general that I accept the criticisms that have been made as rounding out what is necessarily a rather hasty statement of a point of view; to discuss these three theories within what is supposed to be a theoretical twenty minutes is just impossible, and so I did lay myself open to the criticism that both Dr. Meister and Dr. Pilley have made. I think, however, that there is a world of difference between the attitude of the progressive educator toward utilizing the past and the way in which the Hutchins school is using it. For the Hutchins school, you read, you accept this truth that is already defined. But a progressive educator will recognize that in one stage he has utilized the present perhaps too little and in another too much, and so on.

Now then, I go with what Dr. Pilley says about the limitation that you deal with needs alone. I referred to the shift from just interests to needs, partly to show that in the development of progressive education, we have shifted from that early stage in which teachers were discovering for the first time what children are, and recognizing children as persons, and then dealt with their interests because they respected the integrity of the child without sensing that interests are also reflections and reactions to the environment in which the individual lives..

And so they moved in the direction of the needs, trying to identify needs in the sense of this illustration: A man says, "I want a drink; I need a drink." There is a difference there. He may want a drink, and his drinking be an anti-social act, but when he needs a drink, it is not only an urge on the part of his physiological organism but it has a social sanction.

But if you leave it simply to needs and don't go on to what Dr.Pilley stressed, taking children's needs and young people's needs and helping them to realize them and develop their personalities in terms of a scheme of values, you have of course only gone a part of the way.

So this emphasis upon mature personality can become just a phrase and isn't in itself sufficient. It does have the advantage of stressing more than words, verbal education, intellectual education, as we ordinarily conceive of it. It has the emphasis of a balanced personality in which the intellect is operating along with healthy emotional, social development. But of course you have to ask yourself what are the criteria of mature personalities.

I also see the limitation with reference to this emphasis upon postulates. I do not think it is progressive education, however, that is responsible for these young people saying "This is a postulate and that is a postulate, and I can take which one I want."

It seems to me the scientific spirit and the democratic faith recognize that when we speak about relative truth, we mean truth that is related to things that are going on in your environment. You take your postulates at your peril. The postulate that you select has to be with reference to the consequences that are going to follow, the implications, the direction in which it leads.

I was a bit nervous when Dr. Pilley mentioned moral values as something separate from a particular mode of life. I go with him, but not if moral values are outside of human life and the consequences to human life, when you include in human life, as I said, all of these admirable traits and strivings and spiritual longings of human beings. But the democratic point of view, and progressive education insofar as it contributes to it, look to the future.

So the values are the democratic values that I mentioned briefly in answer to Dr. Lindeman's question. The whole movement with which progressive education identifies itself is this movement of emancipation of people so that they are not, let us say, Jews first and individuals second, but they are individuals first, then exploring where respect for the individual and the differences in individuals will lead you.

But that is not sufficient in itself. The way in which you testify to respect for the individual is what that leads you to do in the development of similar distinctive abilities and talents and interests in the lives of others. That makes it a social conception and forces us to deal with the present. But it points in the direction of an increasing respect for the integrity of personality and for experiences shared in this generous way with others.

DR. LINDEMAN: I should like to query Dr. Pilley on this: He is correct in his inference that I was drawing my conclusions about morality from anthropological material rather than from philosophical or theological material, and that I did assume *that,* more or less, is a part of the way people live together; that it doesn't come from on high. The phrase that he used, however, to describe the other theory was moral autonomy, and he equated that with freedom. I should like to have him say a little more about that. I am not sure I understand the sense in which individual or moral autonomy becomes freedom.

DR. PILLEY: To answer the first point I would say that it is in the nature of human beings always to be reaching beyond what exists to something that they value more, and just as in scientific technology new devices have to be conceived in the imagination before they can be constructed, so in the moral sphere better ways of living have to be imaginatively conceived of before they can be striven for. Some minds have a far greater capacity than others for conceiving of what is morally excellent, just as some minds have a far greater capacity for extending scientific understanding. It is such minds that have the greatest contributions to make to the education of others. For my own part I wouldn't want to quarrel with those who speak of new moral, or scientific, insights coming from "on high" though I know that for many the expression has unfortunate associations.

To my mind our moral education consists in our developing new moral insights with the help of the ideas and the example of men of greater moral understanding than ourselves. As teachers therefore we should attach the greatest importance to encouraging in our pupils the kind of imagination necessary for achieving such insights. For this we must respect their ideas even when we are confident that they are wrong. In this our task is not at all that of merely transmitting the cultural habits of the group.

DR. LINDEMAN: From your point of view the opposite of relative morals is not fixed morals?

DR. PILLEY: I believe that some ways of living are better than others—in allowing greater opportunity for the achievement of human excellence—just as in science some conclusions are nearer the truth than others. I am also confident that there are better reasons supporting my belief in what is good than there are in support of some other beliefs—those of the Nazis, to take an extreme example. But that doesn't give me—or anyone else—the right to dogmatize and say "I have the *final* answer." This is as little justified in morals as it is in science and leads to far more deplorable consequences.

But though we should never dogmatize in discussion we can only live moral lives when we have thought enough about our ideals to be confident in them and ready to fight for them when necessary. Today we are showing our faith in democratic principles by fighting for them. It is true that men will fight for all sorts of reasons. A man will fight back when someone hits him on the nose, and that is little more than an animal reaction. A man may also fight for what may seem to be a high ideal but may only be a slogan like that of democracy. But it is only those who have thought out their ideal and are intent upon the kind of moral development necessary for its realization who will show the highest kind of courage in its defense. In this thinking the writings of poets, of philosophers, and of saints have an irreplaceable contribution to make. The Education for Freedom movement with its cult of the 100 Best Books seems to me to have an inkling of this even though its choice of books and its attitude towards them seems to me misguided. Here I might add that it seems to me a great mistake to throw out everything Education for Freedom advocates. The strength of the movement depends in a large measure on the fact that in many things it is half right.

DR. LINDEMAN: I think you can make out a good case that what we assume, from the reading of history, to be the creative idea of some person in the realm of morals is not so at all. It might be, rather, people tried something which actually provided satisfactions, and then someone verbalized it, getting credit for being the inventor of what had grown out of experience.

DR. PILLEY: But the discovery of what is morally excellent isn't the result of blind trial and error any more than scientific discovery is. New ideas of human excellence, like new ideas in art, have their origin in the informed imagination of men of genius. Another thing to remember is that as soon as we get beyond the level of animal satisfaction we find satisfying only the things we have learned to find satisfying. It is only through learning to appreciate things of excellence that they come to bring satisfaction. How would you suggest that people judge what is satisfying?

DR. LINDEMAN: Not by what somebody else said.

DR. PILLEY: I agree that there is in human beings a latent power of discerning and of valuing what is excellent. Even so teachers have an important part to play in helping in the development of that power.

DR. LOWREY: Isn't there an additional step? Doesn't it come to the point where in addition to verbalizing and getting credit for inventions, either that "inventor" or the next fellow says, "This is right, absolutely right, and therefore you"—to someone else who might not quite see it in the same way—"must adhere to it"?

DR. PILLEY: To answer that I must draw a distinction between discussion and action. When we are discussing a question without regard to any immediate action we do not have to commit ourselves to any particular view and there is no excuse for dogmatism. If we are sensible people we will be eager to learn from others and be willing to change our own views. But in a crisis we have to act, and in acting we have to commit ourselves. We have to act as though things that we may not be sure about were true. Without doing that we could not act at all. In the present conflict with the Nazis we are fighting in defense of our democratic faith. We may be wrong about the conception of democracy we are fighting for and in discussion we should be prepared to admit it. In the meanwhile we have to fight for what we believe as the best we know.

DR. LINDEMAN: I was a little disturbed by Dr. Meister's saying, if I understood him correctly that the chief barrier to further gains, or the impediment which now faces us in making our education better, is the bigness and the administrative rigidity of the public school system. At that point he left me a little confused, because he seemed to say that the answer was a higher degree of professionalization among teachers. How would that solve the problem?

MR. MEISTER: First I should like to say, before tackling that question directly, that many of us in public school work feel that discussions of this kind are so often unrealistic. Of what avail is it for us to straighten out our ideas to the last minutia unless we can attack the forces that are operating today to undermine the principles of democratic faith in which we believe, because these forces are much smarter than we are and take advantage of the inherent difficulties in working in a large system?

The answer in part lies in a greater devotion to professionalism on the part of the workers who profess this faith. The number of these workers is large indeed, but they choose to wait for other things to be set right before sacrificing the extra energy needed to solve the problem.

That is to say, we encounter an attitude on the part of professional workers which insists upon a bigger educational budget "before I will go beyond the formula of service I am required for." It results in an unwillingness, for example, to set up new precedents because that violates a formula of service. As a result, Rome burns while we fiddle around. We live our lives in two parts. We live up to the letter of the law during our so-called professional lives, and then we live our lives as persons afterwards.

DR. THAYER: Isn't it a question of fighting on a number of fronts at once, not just a second front, because if you develop this professional attitude that Mr. Meister speaks of, you make it more and more evident that the type of mass education that is forced upon you is imposed in the light of what constitutes a professional point of view?

That is why I stress the fact that the progressive point of view recognizes the importance of children as persons. Now this whole movement that I call Education for Adjustment is designed to solve the problems of mass education according to certain superficially arrived-at scientific procedures. They were "demonstrating" for a while that you could teach large classes as effectively as small classes because they reduced everything to this narrow procedure of skills and study guides and the like. But when you recognize that the pupils are persons, that they are different, not only does your professional practice change but you will not tolerate the budgets that make inevitable these large classes. As I say, we have to fight along these different fronts.

Take the contribution that the psychiatrists have to give. How many adults could work for the number of hours in the school day with as many people in the same room under the conditions that we ask children to work in a public school? Just think of what it would do to you to be with a crowd hour after hour, day after day. As soon as you begin to get under the skin of children and see them as persons, I say that you would consider that intolerable as a program for a board of education or as a program for teaching in a school.

MR. MEISTER: I have one more thought. I believe that discussions of this kind tend to grow unrealistic if we do not consider the implications for the masses of children. If we believe, for example, that we can have a healthier citizenry if ninety percent of our citizens know more about the workings of their bodies, then we must also grant that we will have a more democratic society if ninety percent of our people learn the meanings of this faith.

Now it must be done in the mass situations. It can be done nowhere else if we are to make progress.

6

WHAT CONSTITUTES A LIBERATING EDUCATION?

JOHN HERMAN RANDALL, JR., *Professor of Philosophy, Columbia University, Chairman.*
COMFORT A. ADAMS, *Professor Emeritus of Electrical Engineering, Harvard University.*
HARRY J. CARMAN, *Dean, Columbia College.*
A. D. HENDERSON, *President, Antioch College.*
HENRY MARGENAU, *Associate Professor of Physics, Yale University.*
DONALD A. PIATT, *Professor of Philosophy, University of California in Los Angeles.*

DR. RANDALL: *What do we want any genuine education to do in a democratic society like ours, in a society into which there has entered so deeply the promise of the scientific spirit? The challenge to be genuinely liberating demands, obviously, the exploring of a great many other possibilities than those which have been traditionally known as the "liberal arts." This challenge to face the future and reconsider our aims and resources is one of the most stimulating and hopeful features in our present situation.*

When we ask, "What does it mean for an education to be genuinely liberating?" we are led to the further questions, "liberation from what?" and "liberation of what?" For any kind of liberty, we now realize, is not merely negative; it demands the active fostering of something. Nor can we consider ends without means. So the questions "liberation from what?" and "liberation of what?" are at once followed by the practical question, "liberation by what?"

I suspect that many backward-looking souls today, when they talk about a liberal education, really mean an education that will liberate people from all new and disturbing ideas. And there are some who clearly mean an education that will liberate those who have suffered it from any concern with the scientific spirit. One of these refugees from science, who eagerly put forth a panacea recently, makes clear his fears in an early chapter. The great difficulty into which our education has got us in our present generation, he discovers, comes from the fact that, steadily and surely and with insidious advance, "scientific method has been encroaching upon thought." Obviously, for this nostalgic gentleman, a liberal education must liberate "thought" from any traffic with scientific method.

Do we really want our education to "liberate" us from the best our present world has to offer, the scientific spirit and the democratic faith? Or do we want it to use these forces to set us free? This is the kind of question we have under advisement here. We are certainly not suffering from any dearth of plans. Each of us has a good specific for some one of the ills to which our educational system is heir: each of us is promoting his own remedy as a kind of cure-all. In themselves, all these schemes hold a great deal of promise. They are all possible means of liberating us from things we should like to be liberated from. I should be surprised if, out of the discussion, there did not emerge the conviction that a large part of the reason why these schemes have been captured by people who are interested in liberating us from things we do not want to be liberated from, is their concentration upon some one plan, one single formula, by which all is to be set right.

THE ARGUMENT
A. D. Henderson

To answer the question: "What Constitutes a Liberating Education?" one must first ask what being liberated means. I assume men are free when they have become masters of themselves, of the forces of nature, and of their own destinies as communities of men. They have become masters of themselves when they have learned to utilize harmoniously and creatively their own individual abilities—intellectual, physical, and emotional. They have become masters of nature when they have freed themselves from superstitions, and in proportion as they understand nature and can harness its forces. They have become masters of their destinies as communities of people when they have learned how to plan and organize cooperatively for the future so as to achieve the greatest possible human happiness.

These generalizations need to be made more specific through a few illustrations. People are free insofar as they possess the tools of learning and techniques of action: the ability to verbalize, to calculate, to analyze and synthesize, to create, to organize, and to administer. People are free who possess, or know how to acquire, the available knowledge pertinent to the courses of action which they are undertaking at the moment. Persons are not free who are handicapped with unnecessary psychological inhibitions, who are the victims of preventable communicable diseases, who harbor irrational prejudices against men of differing views or other cultures or other races, or who practice religious bigotry. People become free as they learn how to organize into social groups to secure, on a basis of equality of opportunity for all men, such advantages as adequate physical comfort, health services, educational opportunity, and economic justice, and also leisure time for cultural pursuits. Achievements such as these bring about liberation. Men have become free in proportion to their attainment of goals such as these. That education is liberating which aids in this process.

At first glance, it might seem that all of education is liberating. But is it? The Nazi method of fomenting racial antagonisms is not liberating; neither is the teaching by the fundamentalists that men are inhibited by original sin; nor are the nationalistic distortions of the facts of history; nor is the teaching of economics as a dogma instead of a vast science of which we are learning only the rudiments. These teachings are not liberating because they are not consistent with the best available knowledge, or because they close the door to the discovery of new knowledge. Hence they tend to limit man's understanding of himself and his environment, and lead to courses of action which do not in the long run have social justification.

It has been suggested by some educators that the study of the greatest books produced in the past constitutes the most truly liberating education. There is certain merit in the contention. These books tend to be comprehensive in their treatment and interpretation of human experience; they help provide good historical perspective; and because they represent the best thinking of their respective times they are useful in understanding how men have attacked the essential problems of their own generations.

But the too exclusive devotion of the student's time to the study of the great books seems to me to be seriously limiting. It causes much time to be spent upon the presentation of many facts (in anthropology and geology, for example) which have been disproved, and of ideas which have been sloughed off as men have made new discoveries. It subjects the student to large doses of opinion which since the time of the writers have been shown to be dogmatic. It places the student in an artificial environment because the world of these books was not the world of today. There is one possibility that setting up these books as the curriculum can do grave harm: if the teacher assumes that they reveal for all time the best possible statements of the ultimate truths that men are seeking. When this happens, the "great books" become another authoritarian approach to education and are the direct antithesis of educating for freedom.

However, properly employed, the great books of the past do constitute one of the primary sources of knowledge available to the true scholar. He is saved much time and labor by taking advantage of the observations which have been screened through many minds. If the product of his thinking is to be some increment to knowledge, he must know what has been known before. Through these studies, the student will get evidence that will aid in maturing his judgment concerning the ethical direction of society. The accumulated wisdom gained from past human experience is undoubtedly an important element in a liberating education. But it is not the sole element.

The great scholars of former ages were concerned with the essential problems of their own times. For examples, when Copernicus described his new system of astronomy, when Locke propounded his views on the natural rights of men, when Darwin formulated the theory of evolution, when Marx outlined his ideas for a socialized economy, each was dealing with a crisis in men's beliefs or with a practical problem in human relations that had validity for the society of the day. The lesson to learn from this is that the students of today—at least the ones with the highest intellectual gifts—should be studying the essential problems of the world today. Indeed, I see in this suggestion a focal point for the reorganization of liberal education.

One way of sensitizing the student to the human problems of his time is through giving him experience in the world about him. Educative experience will give him sensitivity toward human needs and aspirations, increase his factual knowledge and his ability to observe facts, demonstrate to him the importance of checking assumptions through practical observations through trial and error, and motivate him for constructive work in society.

Another element in a liberating education for today is our willingness to draw upon the experience of other national and racial groups contemporary with our own. Society today, throughout the world, is closely interdependent. Discoveries in science occur irrespective of cultural boundary lines, as do also developments in the social, economic, and political fields. As a nation, we shall find ourselves lagging in cultural advancement if we fail to take full advantage of the knowledge gained through other nations' scientific and social experimentation. The too strict worship of our little body of Western knowledge can lead to intellectual inbreeding and sterility.

A liberating education, then, is an exploring education. The student seeks wisdom wherever wisdom can be found—in the record of the experience of the past, in the accounts of contemporary experience, and in his own participation in the world about him. The student searches for knowledge on the theory that the whole truth, even in matters spiritual, has not yet been discovered. He uses the scientific method. Knowledge becomes dynamic, like the kind of world we live in. The scientific spirit and method are essential to a liberating education.

In this approach to learning, how does the student discover the values by which he will live and work? The central issue between the Neo-Thomists and their challengers probably lies in the method by which each determines values. The former group assumes the presence of values which transcend human experience; they appear to assume that these values have been revealed through the writings of the great philosophers and that since human nature (supposedly) does not change, these statements of values are good for all time. The second group assumes that the scholars of today and of the future, using the accumulated evidence and the more rigorous techniques of thinking that were unavailable in the past, can provide progressively better expositions of fundamental values than have been provided heretofore.

Men must makes choices in determining their future courses of action, and these choices must be based upon what to the individual are fundamental values. These values, I think, can be found only through analyzing human experience. Those who have made such analyses before can, of course, aid us greatly in our thinking. Experience also aids in showing when action is good or bad. Out of experience the human race learns to set up value-scales such as honesty and dishonesty, temperance and intemperance, justice and injustice, tolerance and intolerance, good will and ill will, on which actions can be contrasted and weighed. The applications of these values may change—as, for example, whether it is good or bad to garden on Sunday, or to engage a neighboring country in war—but in making new ventures or new experiments the orientation to past experience remains, and hence judgments can be made about the ethical directions for the future.

Does this view leave the human race adrift without any moorings? It does not necessarily deny the existence of a fundamental purpose in life. But as far as the human race is concerned, that purpose may be emergent, and our concept of that purpose can be continually enlarged. For example, new views about the nature of man and his potentialities in life have been opened up by the fairly contemporary writings of Darwin, Marx, Freud, and Veblen. The impact of these views upon education has been profound, and has stimulated a whole new surge of learning. Yet it would be limiting, rather than liberating, men's future to assume that there is any *final* finality about the conclusions of these men. Part of the function of a liberating education is to enable the individual to make his own analysis of human experience and determine by his own reason what he considers, for the present, a socially justifiable course of action.

In conclusion, I would define a liberating education as one that serves the function in society of helping to liberate men from ignorance, superstition, fear, prejudice, unnecessary physical handicaps, and the need to use force in trying to solve recurring social crises. More positively, I would define it as the education that helps produce men who because of their perspective of human experience, their sensitivity to the limiting forces of the time, and their knowledge of social dynamics, can aid in advancing human progress.

THE DISCUSSION

DR. ADAMS: To me education implies that training of the mind which will make it most effective in the solution of those numerous and vital problems involved in the evolution of human society.

To this end I shall make an arbitrary subdivision of these problems into three groups, although they are closely intertwined in the overall perspective.

1. The problems involved in the field of applied science, including engineering.

2. Problems in economics, which although they cannot always be stated with the same definiteness as those of physical science, nevertheless are subject to a few simple laws such as that of supply and demand. The solution of this group of problems is often of more vital interest to the general welfare and happiness of society at large than is true of the scientific or engineering problems.

3. Problems involving human relationships or human conduct. These are the most fundamental of all and unfortunately the ones which receive the least attention in our educational system as it now operates.

Although our educational system has been fairly effective in connection with the solution of the physical or engineering problems, there is now ample evidence available to prove without a shadow of a doubt that it has been woefully deficient in connection with the solution of the problems of the other two groups.

For example, consider the following pictures in the economic field:

1. The economy of the United States in 1933: A nation with abundant natural resources; production machinery sufficient to produce three times the actual output of that year; at least twelve million workers out of jobs, although willing and anxious to work the idle machinery in order to produce the things which they needed and wanted to consume; hunger, poverty, and discouragement amongst millions of industrious citizens, while other millions were living in luxury or comfort.

2. Compare the above picture with that of the present date. With at least ten million less available workers we are producing approximately four times the wealth per annum, and although a considerable part of this wealth is being used for purposes of destruction, there has never been a period in the history of this country when the people as a whole lived so well as they do today.

Can any thinking person view these two pictures without being forced to the conviction that something is terribly wrong with our economic system and therefore with the education which underlies it?

Consider next the more fundamental question of human relationships as related to the present world chaos. Although I realize the economic basis of the present war, that is secondary to the underlying laws of human relationships. In a world which is as a whole poor, from the material point of view, we are witnessing the wanton destruction of a total amount of physical wealth which is several times the present capital wealth of this rich country. Can anyone view this picture without the conviction that there is something terribly lacking in the education, not only of our masses, but of our leaders and so-called statesmen, most of whom have been exposed to the best that our educational system affords?

The major defect in our educational method is that we do not teach our young people to think logically for themselves. We cram their minds with information, most of it superficial and un-coordinated. We train their memories. We make them orthodox in this field or that, but we do not train them to think logically without bias on any subject.

The field in which this defect is apt to be least prominent is that of science and technology, although even there, there is a strong tendency to a kind of orthodoxy that costs the industries of this country many millions of dollars every year.

Let me illustrate. About forty years ago I was asked to design an electric motor for a specific and unusual purpose. The three largest manufacturers of electric machines in this country had failed, with only such information as was supplied to them by the user, but not because they could not have designed a satisfactory machine with complete information. In short, the user did not know enough about the requirements to write intelligent specifications. The three manufacturers accepted without question the guess of the users as to the proper rating of the machine. Finding that I could not get the information which was necessary for an intelligent design, I spent a week in the plant of one of the large users and acquired a fund of information, and a perspective of the problem which was sufficient for the purpose. This information not only made possible the design of a suitable motor but also doubled the output of a single machine and revolutionized the technique which had been orthodox in that industry for thirty years. I could cite numerous similar cases, in one of which the output was multiplied by eight.

In other words, I only did exactly what every logician must do if he expects to solve his problem. Any logical conclusion is sound only under two conditions: First, the premises must be not only accurate but comprehensive, and second, the logic must be sound. The logic may be sound and the premises accurate but if the latter are incomplete the conclusions are worthless.

In the case cited above, the three electrical machinery manufacturers accepted without question the superficial and incomplete statement of the premises supplied to them. In this connection it should be noted that the knowledge as to what premises are vital to the problem in hand, or as to what information is necessary for the design of the machine in question, is only available to those who have a thorough knowledge of the laws involved and a clear quantitative perspective of the phenomena involved.

The reason why so few of our engineering experts are competent in this respect is briefly as follows: In college they are rushed through the underlying sciences into the so-called practical problems and are taught the technique of solving them. Unfortunately, every solution of an engineering problem involves approximations from the scientific point of view. The approximations are satisfactory within a certain range of application but useless outside of that range. Thus, as industrial problems become more and more complicated, these conventional solutions such as provided in handbooks, become increasingly dangerous, particularly since the students and often the instructors themselves, are not aware of the approximation involved.

Thus when one of these bright young men tries to use the formulae which he has learned and the answer proves completely defective, he is said to be too theoretical. As a matter of fact, he has no theory worthy of consideration. He is just a technician. He has never known the satisfaction of understanding the fundamental principles, of building his own solution around the particular conditions of each problem. In short, he has never been taught to think for himself.

On the other hand, the real engineer is so hedged about by the laws of nature that he is forced to think straight. He knows that no amount of wishful thinking will avail if he slips, either in the matter of premises or in his logic. Commercial bias can play no part in this type of thinking. . . .

The majority of our citizens are subject to a persistent propaganda of which most of them are wholly unaware. This applies not only to the logic involved, but also to the premises. In other words, our so-called educated people are so completely lacking in the habit of sound and critical thinking that they not only accept incomplete premises but also the logic based on those premises, or in some cases upon assumptions or slogans taken out of the air. They are innocent victims of propaganda which has left such ruts in their minds that even when they are temporarily lifted out of those ruts by unescapable logic, and get a brief view of the outside scenery, the moment the effort is relaxed, they drop back again into the rut of orthodoxy.

If this were a field of minor importance, I would not be so vehement, but most vital questions are facing the world today, and the fork of the road which we take after this war, will determine whether we are to have a good world in which to live, or one dominated by greed and material power which can lead only to a world-wide revolution. We need an education which will fortify our citizens against any persistent propaganda, however plausible it may seem to the unthinking minds. . . .

Our present system fails almost completely to emphasize the importance of sound, clean, honest, and unbiased thinking. It fails also to emphasize the importance and vitality of those basic laws of human relationships which have come down to us through four thousand years of recorded history, from the greatest thinkers, philosophers, teachers, and prophets of all ages, nations, and religions, and as a result of thousands of years of human experience. Some forms of conduct have been found to promote the happiness and welfare of those concerned; other forms, unhappiness. We seem to be ashamed of these principles of human decency, which are often referred to as "soft, sentimental, or idealistic" by those who pride themselves on being realists. They seem to forget that these principles or laws of human relationships are simple common sense and logical conclusions based upon the most comprehensive premises.

DR. MARGENAU: Let us consider some of the positive values that accrue from a study of science. First, *science liberates from ossified preconception.* It leads the way from witchcraft to social enlightenment, from quackery to medicine, from astrology to astronomy, and so forth.

Secondly: *science achieves liberation from drudgery.* That, also, is a commonplace which needs no further emphasis here.

A third fact, which I believe is not as generally recognized but states one of the chief liberating functions of science, is this: *Science frees from the tyranny of words.* Everybody who has taken a course in an exact science knows the meticulous emphasis which is placed on precise definition, on stability in the usage of terms. I suggest you endeavor to define such words as "freedom." Try to define freedom in a manner acceptable to all, acceptable to all Americans, acceptable to all nations. Try to define "democracy." I know these are heretic suggestions, but unless we face these problems we shall never achieve what they imply.

The *humanizing effect of science* is well-known. Science cuts across nations, racial groups. Hitler, in establishing his tyranny, first of all proceeded to eliminate from Germany many good theoretical scientists and mathematicians. After their removal his movement succeeded in unfolding itself.

What are we to do about the teaching of science in colleges and schools? As a preliminary let us ask what is the matter with present teaching of science? How can it be brought more closely into harmony with the potential good which, according to the foregoing remarks, resides in it.

First, I believe that the elementary courses taught on the college level, and also on the secondary school level, are too full. They prevent their unhappy victims from seeing the woods because of the trees; they obscure the niceties of method in a welter of useful but uninteresting facts. In our elementary courses in chemistry and physics, we show the students too many gadgets, and often take excessive pride in purely manipulatory skill.

In the second place, we have catered only to two extreme types of interest, and this is particularly true in physics. We have tried to make either engineers or mathematicians of our students. Why engineers or mathematicians only? Is there not a large body of central interest in philosophy and history which we should endeavor to satisfy? That, I believe, must be done in any reasonable post-war program for education if it is to be successful. There are, of course, very noteworthy material deficiencies in elementary school and secondary school teaching. I think it should be stated with emphasis that no science program, no program of liberal education, can succeed unless the secondary schools do better work in preparing the men who go to college than they have done in the past. . . .

I suggest that we first of all modify elementary college courses taught in the sciences today, in an endeavor to make them more fluid, more thorough, and less inclusive.

In the second place, we must teach the sciences with greater historical perspective. In fact, I think we should require from every teacher of science not only evidence of his proficiency in the technical aspects of his science, but also a thorough knowledge of its history.

We are launched today on the same down-hill course which German science took during the last ten years. The suggestions I have made appear to me to be essential if we wish to erect a barrier which can stop our coasting.

DR. CARMAN: I should like to raise these questions: What are some of the outstanding things which have been accomplished in the United States of America? What are some of the things on the credit side of the ledger? What are some of the items on the debit side of the ledger? In what direction ought we to be going? What should be the world of tomorrow? What should be our place in that world of tomorrow? What can we do about it all, from the point of view of a liberating education?

On the credit side of the ledger, at the head of the list, I would place freedom—not absolute freedom, but freedom to think, believe, speak, and choose. In other words, we have proceeded in this country, it seems to me, on the assumption that human beings have individual minds, wills, and aspirations, and that is what differentiates them from other animals. They have capacities for self-improvement, even if that self-improvement appears at times to be pretty slow. Moreover, we have operated on the basis that human beings should be allowed to use their minds, exercise their wills, and manage their affairs, as a means of learning how to do all of these things better. Exercising one's will and managing one's affairs as a means of learning how to do things better, does not mean that one has absolute freedom, but freedom insofar as one does not tread upon the toes of his fellow beings.

In the second place, we have developed a system of education, faulty though it may be, which assumes that all human beings have moral worth in themselves. I know that assumption cannot be proved absolutely, and yet I am very certain that it underlies our way of life. Our geographical location, our mixture of races and varieties of heritage give us unique aspects for our development.

We have no legalized aristocracy, no military caste, no quasi-military bureaucracy. We instruct our youth in human ideals which form the essence of democracy. We have increasingly sought to enrich the individual's life by instruction in the best creations of men and women in letters, the arts, the sciences, and all the other phases of the human spirit.

In the third place, we have won great victories over political tyranny. Slavery has been ended; the politician is under heavy attack. Freedom of speech, press, religion, trial by jury and the right of habeas corpus are guaranteed. These civil rights or liberties are not yet absolute, yet it would be difficult, it seems to me, to overestimate their importance. They were beacon lights to those millions who left the Old World for the new freedom from oppression, seeking freedom just as other millions would today were it possible for living victims of Hitler's madness to escape.

But there is another side to the ledger. American civilization is far from perfect. Despite the fact we have built a hundred cities and gridironed a continent with rails and motor highways, and conquered stream, forest, and desert, our house is far from being in order. We have pillaged and wasted our natural resources; we have shamelessly exploited a large percentage of our population. Slums and other wretched habitations feature our urban communities. Consumers of our goods have been, and still are, defrauded. Racial minorities, especially the Negro, suffer a thousand and one humiliations.

The things which have increasingly given us mastery over the physical universe tend to enslave us because of our failure to date to utilize them more fully for the benefit of humanity. Religious bigotry is still prevalent. Our national income is badly distributed. I could go on.

Why this debit side of the ledger? Largely because we have given material acquisition precedence over human welfare. Too many Americans have allowed themselves to become spiritually bankrupt. No institution is better than the persons who are responsible for its functioning. Whatever else we profess to be, we are born pragmatists. We are a materialistic people. The great majority of our forebears, who came to these shores to improve their social or economic status by means of hard work, endless planting, and technical ingenuity, proceeded to exploit. Values were expressed in terms of money, of personal advantage, and not in terms of the acquisition and the refinement of standards, physical, emotional, or spiritual. Success in life meant getting on in a material way. It was very natural that it should be so. In the past the territorial growth of the United States, its vast stretches of fertile lands, its rich natural resources, the overlapping waves of immigrants continually providing a new bottom layer for the social structure, and the rise of new industries, have often combined to make it easy to rise from office boy to a captain of industry or an economic prince. Today, as the nation grows older, the proportion of each generation who can realize such a dream will probably become smaller. It seems to me that the time must come when these material values should be replaced by other values in life.

This nation is now at the parting of the ways. We must make a choice between things spiritual and things material. We must decide whether we will place our emphasis upon rational and human ends, or upon Mammon. We must decide whether we will make things economic an end in themselves, or a means to an end. We must decide whether, individually and nationally, we are going to put a premium on selfishness, prejudice, bigotry, and racial antagonism, or upon the doctrine of the brotherhood of man, not only in theory but in practice.

We must decide whether the United States is to play an imperial role and exploit the rest of the world, and thus run the almost certain risk of becoming the most hated nation on the face of the earth, or whether this country will collaborate with other nations in establishing an international authority which will have a jurisdiction over those matters of concern to all nations.

Finally we must make up our minds whether the forces of reaction or those of liberalism are to prevail. By liberalism I mean a course of action which promotes the welfare of the masses of our citizenry, and not a favored few. The time has gone by when the masses can be persuaded to believe that poverty, anxiety, and living in a constant state of fear are in accordance with God's will. Through the schools, the press, and the radio, they have been made aware of their power to organize for the defense of what they regard as their interest and their rights as human beings.

Unquestionably, man will continue to gain control over the physical world. The great technical revolution which features our age will not terminate with the war. Gadgets and machines will not only enable us to improve our standard of living, but at the same time give us more leisure for living. The world of tomorrow, the product of the scientific, humanistic, rationalistic, and democratic revolutions of the last four hundred years, should be a world of freedom and control, not only freedom of religion, of speech, of organization, of learning, of opportunity of enterprises, but a world where society, through government, will prevent monopolization and other economic ills, anti-social in character. In the world of tomorrow, certainly more people should be free, free in the sense that President Henderson has set forth.

Any educational scheme which we devise should be an educational scheme which will not only promote those freedoms which President Henderson suggests, but one which will enable us to put our house in order and rid it of all those things which are on the debit side of the ledger. I am not a pessimist; I am not a rumor monger—I am a practising historian. History, it seems to me, should not be just a compilation of facts; it should give us vision, viewpoints, and perspective. As such, history points the direction in which we have been going to date. Unless we do set our house in order, we are in for trouble. I would have that liberating education which President Henderson sets forth save us that trouble.

DR. PIATT: The academic mind is notoriously more at home in the abstract discussion of problems than in the concrete action of solving them, and even the most pragmatically minded educators run the danger of making aspiration and inspiration a substitute for rather than a stimulus and guide to future action. Our main job lies ahead of us in following through the implications of liberal education for action, and the context of our day-to-day work will be very different from, and much less favorable than the context of our meetings here. Are we ready to meet that challenge?

It does not take much thought or analysis to see that education has failed because it has been primarily technical, vocational, and professional rather than esthetic, moral, and religious. The need for a knowledge of values as directing objectives is a piously empty platitude. The difficult question concerns the most reliable way or agency for ascertaining this knowledge, and it concerns the relation between knowledge of values and knowledge of "facts." Our first task in qualifying as liberal educators is to clear up the tragic confusion enveloping the word "knowledge" when we refer to moral knowledge, or more widely to knowledge of values. The first lesson we have to learn is that we mean either *scientific* knowledge or something that is not knowledge at all but a pretender that has to masquerade as knowledge in order to gain credence.

The plain truth is that the failure of education has brought us to a point where we must courageously face an issue that we have not wanted to face. Power and responsibility should be correlative, and power has been transferred in our society from the churches to the schools, without the correlative transfer of moral responsibility. It should now be clear to everybody that secular education means scientific education, and that it cannot mean anything else. That should be clear but it isn't. Too many "educators" still think that responsibility for higher values stems from and centers in the church, if indeed they think much about this at all, and that it is only responsibility for a knowledge of "facts" that resides in the schools and belongs to science. These sophists, as a Socrates or Plato would justly call them, refuse to accept the implications and consequences of the power that has been granted them.

The situation in which we find ourselves is so confused that it is difficult to find words that will clarify it because even the best of our words·are charged with the habitual meanings that we need to dispel. Thus I have been wanting to say that all truly liberal education is moral education and that this is one and the same as scientific education. This makes sense rather than contradiction only when we succeed in disengaging science as the experimental method (and the only method that has proved dependable) of converting private opinions into public knowledge, from "science" as a special and peculiarly appropriate subject-matter. Our verbal habit of equating science with "natural" science, and morals with some extra-natural authority or revelation or faith has to be overcome. Until we look upon all values as human and fallible valuations, until we regard them with the same distrust and critical scrutiny relative to their claims and evidence or justification for their claims that a physicist employs as a matter of course toward his facts, hypotheses, and laws, education will continue to be haphazard and irresponsible.

There is of course an intelligible and tenable reason for thinking of the "natural" sciences when we think of science, and for the divisions of the university curriculum into the humanities or "liberal" arts and the sciences. But the tenable reasons for the divisions and subdivisions, for the ever-increasing specialization in education, are quite different from and are obscured by the' untenable reasons that are commonly accepted. The similarities and the interrelations of departments and of groupings of departments are now much more in need of emphasis than the differences. And this emphasis requires clear recognition of the sense in which every subject in the curriculum is, or means to be, equally a science—a *natural* science—and an art. The tenable reasons for dividing fields of study refer to differences in subject-matter, differences that require different kinds of procedural analysis. A life-science has to use and develop methods that differ from those of a physical science for the simple reason that living bodies behave differently from inanimate bodies. Similarly, a valuational science has to construct methods that are adapted to the complexities of human valuational behavior.

But this statement of the differences reveals rather than conceals the unity of the scientific or knowledge-seeking enterprise, and helps to make clear the sense in which every study is both a science and an art, a liberating art. We carry over the inveterate habit of conceiving science, science at its best, "natural" science, as a disclosure of Being, or of the world as it is apart from human intervention, apart from art. That is, we set up a dualism of man and the world, on the one side of which is man the transformer, the producer, the artist or artisan; on the other side is Nature or Matter, a realm of being fixed by immutable laws, utterly independent of man's wishes, purposes, and endeavors. Man is in some sense *in* this world but not *of* it. Natural science so interpreted is alien to art, is the antithesis of art. Natural laws implacably stand off against human hopes, against human values. On this view, man's choice is clear: either be intelligent, realistic, scientific, and take the world on its own terms, acquiesce, bow down before the inevitable; or retreat into a spiritual asylum, seek the edification of the liberal arts, hope without thinking, live and die with grace, dignity, and beauty. Such is the mockery of a "liberal" education.

The task of liberal education is to correct this criminal absurdity by show-ing that only liberating arts are sciences and that only sciences are liber-ating arts, and that all sciences are natural sciences. Physics ceased to be bad metaphysics and became a (natural) science precisely when it became an experimental art. This means that physics began—what it is up to the social and value-sciences to finish—to treat man's activities as an indigenous part of nature's activities: experimental changes purposefully introduced into natural events gave man the power over these events of predicting what changes will occur in nature when other changes in nature are experi-mentally produced. Science was thus *not* a disclosure of ultimate and im-mutable Being but rather prediction of different orders of Becoming or of change. The potentialities of science as a liberating art or as a productive art came more and more into their own as the theoretically possible changes in nature (of pure science) were capitalized to man's advantage in tech-nology or applied science. Human engineering became entirely feasible. Man had found the way to make natural mechanisms effectuate his purposes without clearly seeing (owing to entrenched habits of mind) the moral and religious import of what he had done. Instead of being "mechanical" and resistant and antithetical to purpose, mechanisms became the natural and the dependable means of realizing purposes. Through man's creative in-telligence, through nature as art, nature's process often came to beneficent fruition. When man resolutely regards himself in his entirety as in and of nature he is on the way to making himself feel at home in nature.

So much for the thesis that a genuine science is a liberating art, and for that part of our thesis that it is vicious to divide our curriculum into the sciences and the arts. Henceforth when we speak of the values of science we will know what we mean, and we can easily answer the objection that values belong to art. About the other part of our thesis, that only sciences are liberating arts, we can be brief. For all that we mean is that liberal art studies are presumably as much a knowledge-seeking inquiry as physics is, and hence that these studies accomplish their purpose in proportion to their success in developing scientific methods and procedures relevant to their subject-matter. The "liberal" arts will live up to their name when and only when they come to be treated scientifically, when they cease to pass off as knowledge that which is nothing but feeling or intuition or vested tradi-tion or authority.

This divorce of science and art in education helps to explain why our universities have provided technical and professional training rather than a liberal education, and it helps us to see more clearly what is wrong with mere technique. The point of indicting the divorce of science and art be-comes sharp and clear when we say that we have divorced the means and the ends of human living. A mere technician is one who is skilled in the use of means for achieving a given end. Since his concern is simply with the means, and not at all with the ends save proximately, save as the assigned end happens or does not happen, he actually does not know what he is doing. He neither knows nor of course feels the significance of his activity. His activity is simply instrumental; he is a tool or a slave, a highgrade tool perhaps but still a tool. Germany through two world wars should be a standing lesson to us of how such "human" tools can be exploited by "leaders" and by a privileged social class. Separate means from ends and what you get is a society in which the masses are the means to the ends of the minority group in power.

Technicians are liberally educated and not just trained, not by studying some "liberal art" on the side, but by learning the purposes and values that alone can socially or culturally justify their technique or profession. They must be taught that the means they are employing may have many social consequences other than that of the assigned end, and that the nature of these consequences may make them too costly a price to pay for the end in question. They must be taught to question the given end, not only by balancing it against the aforesaid other consequences of their action, but by evaluating it in the light of its own social consequences. They must be made to see, what all too few see, that what people do determines what they are, that conduct determines character. The moral values of free enterprise appear very differently when we consider not simply the quantity and the kind of "goods" but also the quantity of the kind of people it produces. Sociologists and psychiatrists are making this point tellingly in dwelling on the theme of frustration and aggression and the neurotic personality of our time.

We have considered the divorce of means and ends from the merely technical standpoint of mere means. Let us now consider it from the standpoint of the ends. It happens that as a professor of philosophy it is a central part of my job to instruct students in scientific inquiry regarding moral ends or values. I want to impart here, if I can, something of the sense of futility and frustration that a teacher of ethics must at times feel.

The teacher of ethics feels walled in and shut off from the factual realities of psychology and the social sciences that alone can provide him with significant moral problems and subject-matter. His impossible job is to teach ethics in a curriculum in which economics is economics, psychology is psychology, public administration is public administration, business is business, and ethics is ethics. Such a division of labor may have seemed to make sense in a pre-industrial age when moral ends could still be conceived as otherworldly, but the only ends that are morally significant in the non-verbal conduct of most people today involve at every turn economic, psychological, sociological, and other considerations that are supposed even by educators to lie outside of ethics. Interrelated phases of the same activity are supposed to be different activities. But surely it ought to be elementary common sense that if values are ends, they are ends of the specific means employed to secure them, and that it is idle to consider ends in abstraction from means. I submit that we cannot get good economics or good ethics until as economists we try to answer the question, "What is our economic system for?" and until as ethicists we answer the question, "What economic conditions are so fixed that we have to accept them, which conditions are susceptible to change, and in what direction and for what purpose should we change them?"

The most acute challenge, then, to liberal education is the urgent need for a broader and more realistic comprehension of morals. The division of the curriculum into departments has made most university students feel that a study of ethics is relatively unimportant in their education and in getting on in the world in which they live. And the ablest of those students who elect the study of ethics are amazed that a curriculum could be planned in such a way that economists may tell them that ethical questions should not be intruded into a class in economics, and that if they are interested in "ideals" they should take a course in ethics. The students were of course naïve in supposing that the curriculum as we now have it was planned; if it were planned, and the moral function of education were taken seriously, all the so-called social sciences would deliberately operate as moral sciences, being differentiated and integrated in terms of interpenetrating phases of means-ends-activities or continua. Economics would be no mere science of wants and the production of satisfaction of wants; aspirations would count as peculiar wants; wants would themselves be evaluated in terms of their broad social consequences; satisfactions would be viewed as to whether they are really satisfactory, and so on. I have singled out economics simply as a forcible illustration, but if we had time to consider current legal education, the kind of lawyers law schools are turning out, or the kind of education dispensed in almost any of the social-procedural departments, we would see that social policy administration is aimed to satisfy private rather that public or moral interests. Ethics has been relegated to the antiquarian study of a disembodied soul and of ideals in vacuo.

There is another aspect of our emphasis on technique that deserves comment. Long ago John Dewey warned us against the tyranny of words. Outside of the laboratory sciences, education has been mainly verbal. Back of the lecture-system of instruction and of the system of written or oral examinations is the seldom criticized assumption that words are embodiments of meanings, that the meaning of the word lies within the word itself. If the student is adept in memory of lectures and assigned readings, and can repeat the magic words or, better yet, can find synonyms for them, it is assumed that he has a real and not just a verbal knowledge of the subject.

If pressed on the point, the instructor would probably admit that words are meaningful as they designate things and situations that are not words and as they are instrumental to non-verbal actions that deal with these things and situations. He ought then to admit that, if words are instruments, there is no sure way of telling whether the student or even the instructor understands, to say nothing of knowing the truth or falsity of, his words until he has tried out the plan of action called for by the words in question. A liberal education will be thing-minded or rather activity-minded and not word-minded. We ought to provide laboratories for every subject so that we can deal directly with our subject-matter and test the truth-value of our words. And since in some subjects this is difficult to do, we ought, especially in these but as far as possible in all, to use words that will picture in imagination and memory the actual situations and problems and activities to which our words refer. And we ought at every step to show what difference our words make to the student's conduct and life outside the class room.

In asking why teaching has on the whole been pretty formal and empty, we come upon another challenge to liberal education. We have not achieved a proper balance between research and teaching. In most universities academic promotion depends on research or rather on published writings, not on the quality of teaching. The former rather than the latter is taken as the test of scholarship. This trend has gone so far that there attaches to the good teacher the suspicion, at the very least, that he is not a scholar. If he inspires his students by making his subject significant, if he is interested in his students as a vital part of his subject, he is likely to be accused of a lack of academic dignity. We shall not solve this problem until we offer adequate inducements to good teaching and until we see that teaching is both a vital form of research and the test of other research. Scientific inquiry is objective and cooperative, not an arm-chair study in solitary confinement, and a free give-and-take between instructor and students is a good cure for pedantry.

One of the worst aspects of the merely research-habit of mind when carried over into teaching is its pseudo-quality of disinterestedness or objectivity. The obligation to be objective is thought to imply absence of emotion and a non-committal attitude on controversial questions. But surely a disinterested attitude is not uninterested. And in those subjects that patently have human desires and emotions and valuations as a substantial part of their subject-matter, an uninterested attitude is not only uninteresting but uninstructive and irrelevant. It ignores or falsifies the facts to be studied. The obligation to be disinterested means properly only to give all the interests at stake a fair and impartial hearing, and to manifest an inclusive but discriminating interest that will do this. The instructor's sense of the importance of his subject he can neither have nor express save in terms of interest. And if he has only thoughts but no convictions, his students will not respect him, nor will they carry anything of lasting value away from his teaching.

Finally, a word concerning the utter absurdity of the view that a teacher should be non-committal on controversial questions. The air of security that surrounds the position of the academic profession befogs the academic mind. In dealing with purely conceptual problems in the comfort of one's library or within the protecting walls of a classroom, it is all too easy to suspend judgment, to see all sides of a question, to keep looking for further evidence, to know that not all the evidence is in and that the available evidence is inconclusive, and hence to make no decision. It is easy to rest on general principles and thus to preserve one's scientific integrity. But if a liberal education is to liberate the conduct of human life, general theories have to prove their value in supplying answers to specific practical problems where of course the evidence is not all in but where decisions nevertheless have to be made, and where they should be made intelligently. Not absolute truth but probability is the guide of life. Decisions on controversial questions have to be made, if not by the instructor, certainly by the less protected student. And a world at war, a bewildered people, despairing of any possibility of an enduring peace, is losing its faith in intelligence precisely because the educator seems to have nothing to say on the burning questions of the day, because theory balks at problems that are practical and pressing.

If educators could feel the temper of our people, if they knew what students say about their teachers, things that are anything but flattering, educators would reconsider very soberly what they are trying to do and what they are actually doing. Higher education has discredited traditional values and standards of value without accepting responsibility for new values and standards. Whether educators are willing to regard their function as religious turns perhaps on their reaction to the word "religious." But certainly a liberating education must supply a rational faith for living.

7

VOCATIONAL EDUCATION: FOR FREEDOM OR FOR DOMINATION?

J. RAYMOND WALSH, *Educational Director, CIO, Chairman.*

DONALD BRIDGMAN, *American Telephone and Telegraph Company.*

EDWIN A. BURTT, *Professor of Philosophy, Cornell University.*

ABBA LERNER, *Professor of Economics, New School for Social Research.*

THERESA WOLFSON, *Professor of Economics, Brooklyn College.*

THE ARGUMENT
Edwin A. Burtt

EDUCATION FOR DEMOCRACY in America will face its most searching and critical test in the decades following the war. It will face that test on all fronts; among the most important of these is that of vocational education. In a country as highly industrialized as the United States it is inevitable that vocational training should constitute a major part of the formal education received by the vast majority of persons above the grade school level. But for at least two reasons it is bound to occupy a still more important position after the war. One is that many new technical developments have appeared, hitherto not commercially significant, which will undoubtedly be put to use in peace-time industry. These require new skills for their mastery, and in the competition for post-war employment training in these skills will be sought by many who see in them a promising avenue for profitable employment and rapid advancement. The other is that the vast majority of returning service men will use the educational opportunity promised by the government to become trained for some industrial task. Whatever opportunity our educational system has after the war to do what it can do with a vast number of future American citizens will have to be done largely through the medium of vocational training.

No one can contemplate vocational education as it now exists in the light of this challenge without the most serious misgivings. In the presence of the desperate need for the kind of education calculated to produce men and women who can become intelligent citizens in a democratic world order, vocational training as at present practised is with rare exceptions a terribly narrowing rather than broadening and liberalizing study, and on three main counts. It is narrowing, first, because it accepts the limitation of teaching a particular skill rather than seriously attempting to foster the growth of the whole individual. It is not that school administrators or personnel men in industry wish such a limitation—they would prefer that students gain training in the basic academic disciplines, in habits of effective cooperation with others, in resourcefulness, and in understanding of their own powers—but the forces tending to minimize the importance of these matters are too insistent and pervasive. Too often, indeed, even the job which a student is to fill is conceived, in practice, as though it consists merely in the exercise of some limited skill, rather than in terms of the social responsibilities which in fact are involved. It is narrowing, second, because it subtly if not explicitly assumes the validity, even sanctity, of the present economic order. Men and women are trained to fit into positions which industry as now organized, expressing the ethical and social philosophy which now underlies it, has waiting for them to fill. In being prepared for these positions they are also encouraged to accept unquestioningly this organization, rather than to participate courageously in its transformation into a more humane and democratic system of economic relationships. It is narrowing, third, because it ordinarily assumes no responsibility to enable the student to see his vocation in its widest social context, that of the living needs of all people throughout the world. So far as any broader purview than that of the local scene plays any part it is apt to be the purview of traditional American imperialism, justifying its exploitations abroad on the plea that a high standard of living at home can only thus be maintained.

How can these serious defects be remedied? How can vocational training be made the medium of education for democratic citizenship in a cooperative world?

One problem is: How far can the new agencies of education that are now growing up, apart from the public and denominational schools and uncontrolled by industry, be reasonably expected to meet this need? I am thinking of such agencies as are being developed by or in support of the trade unions, or by consumer cooperatives. It seems likely, however, that in the post-war decades, at least, the bulk of what is done in this field will be done by the public schools.

Another very vital problem is whether a vocational course itself can be taught in such a way that it becomes a liberating and socializing experience, or whether the only feasible procedure is to combine it externally with courses in history, philosophy, and the arts. So far as I can discover, the latter of these two practices is accepted at the present time with practical unanimity by those who believe in the need of liberal education. Pressure of time and the difficulty of finding adequate motivation in the students, along with other causes, dictate that the courses aiming at the achievement of a certain skill attempt nothing but that achievement; it is left to other studies to give the student whatever sense he may gain of the larger context and serious human responsibilities which the acquisition of that skill involves. But this is quite unsatisfactory for many reasons. It means constant and strong pressure to reduce such cultural accompaniments to the barest minimum. It leaves it to the student to work out, unaided, the bearing of what he learns in his non-technical courses on his career in his chosen vocation.

Worst of all, from the point of view of the problems in educational philosophy that are reflected, it implies that certain subjects—the subjects constituting the bulk of educational content for vast numbers of our citizens—are intrinsically devoid of liberating and humanizing possibilities. But this is a hard conclusion to accept. Just as any subject whatever can be taught in a deadening, inhumane, and undemocratic fashion, so it seems that any subject of live human concern ought to be capable of being taught so that it becomes a broadening and enriching force in the lives of those who share the experience. It ought to be possible to teach a vocational skill in such a way that students gain some awareness of its historical background, of the principles of scientific method involved in its development, of the ethical and social problems that appear in connection with its present exercises, of its manifold relationships to other functions and the problem in vocational pedagogy, and how the support of those who would be affected by such a change can be secured over a sufficient period of time to give it serious and systematic trial.

And this question presents us with an equally baffling problem. As I write, I have just come from a conference on the relation between religion and education. As might be expected, nothing approaching general agreement appeared on many of the subjects that came into the discussion. But there was a surprising degree of agreement on this matter: Whatever it seems desirable to do, the practical problem of accomplishing it centers in the securing of teachers who are capable of carrying it out. Where can such teachers be found? What criteria for their selection can be wisely employed? How should they be trained? If these questions pose difficulty in the field of religious education, they pose a still more baffling perplexity in the field which is now being discussed. We not only require a combination of qualifications that are rarely found together, and a varied preparation which few perhaps will have the patience to undertake; but we face the great likelihood that most of those who go through such a course of teacher training would be dissatisfied to use their talents in the vocational field. Persons who now teach vocational subjects in a liberalizing way do so for the most part because of an accidental combination of conditioning factors; had they been trained in their early years to become the kind of teachers they now are they would in many cases have chosen a different career.

A final problem which must not go unmentioned is posed by the serious and growing threat that our educational system may be subjected to some sort of totalitarian control if a democratic solution of these perplexities cannot be quickly found. Would-be authorities, both old and new, are lying in wait to capture American education and prostitute it to their own obscurantist, sectarian, or doctrinaire ends. They know just what they think ought to be done, and will not hesitate to do it if they can persuade us to give them the power. Any such outcome would be no less calamitous to vocational education then to other parts of our present system; it would not only enslave it still more completely to a capitalism as yet essentially unregenerate, but would probably also make it subservient to other undemocratic programs and institutions. By what policies and activities will we be most likely to avert such a tragedy while the foundations of more adequate vocational training are securely established?

THE DISCUSSION

Mr. Bridgman: When I was asked to contribute to this discussion, it seemed to me that it might be worth while to revert to some opinions I secured from personnel men in a number of companies a few years ago. Since that was before the war, I suspect that the war situation has changed the actual working out of these opinions somewhat, but I feel very sure that for a long-time program they represent what these other men in personnel work in industry and I myself would feel were desirable objectives for vocational education which is preparing the young men and women whom they are seeking for their companies.

These are the qualities and the beginning skills which this group of personnel men in industry emphasize. First of all, a very simple sort of thing; good work habits, dependability, and the ability to get on with their fellows; second, a real command of the basic academic skills, such as the use of our language and mathematical accuracy; third, some understanding of their own abilities and interests with relation to broad areas of work, recognition of the value of all sorts of honest work, whether manual or mental, and readiness to enter upon the sort of work for which they are best fitted; finally, familiarity with the tools used in the work to be undertaken and with the atmosphere of shop or office, and a thorough grounding in the methods necessary for the development of some definite skill.

I think everyone would agree that these were desirable traits in young employees, and it may be more worth while to discuss the type of school in which you may find them developed rather than the desirability of the traits themselves.

Good work habits, the ability to get on with one's fellows, would require, it seems to me, a school atmosphere in which there is a sort of constructive orderliness and an opportunity for a sense of achievement in children of all types and levels of intelligence, so that they may have that sense as the basis for a feeling of personal security and worthwhileness. There needs to be in such a school a freedom from group conflict, from discrimination, and from domineering methods.

If we are going to have a real command of academic skills, even the simplest ones, you need the establishment of high academic standards and the development of real incentive in a field which is not obviously vocational.

Some knowledge of his own abilities on the part of the student certainly requires a real interest by the teacher and the school administration in the capacities and desires of each child, and some development of effective counseling methods for the individual child. The child, too, if he is going to see where his own work may fit into that of industry as a whole needs to have some conception of the business structure and the forces at work in it. He must know something about the distribution and requirements of different occupations. I suspect that this is a background that might help to make him a constructive member of a trade union.

The final thing, the desire for some understanding of the atmosphere of shop or office and the tools with which the student will work, is perhaps most noteworthy because of the fact that there is no insistence upon the possession of some specific skill. What is wanted is a notion of a standard of workmanship. Where that is acquired there will be greater flexibility in fitting oneself to different types of jobs rather than to the particular one which the individual may enter at the beginning.

I think we did find that this particular desire was not always shared by some small companies which, very naturally, have need for employees who can fit into the specific jobs that they have available and which may not have the resources and the personnel to give the training in their own work which the larger companies might have. This is, also, the sort of thing which during the war period has been overshadowed by the need, even of large companies, particularly in the war production field, to secure a large number of people equipped to do a particular thing immediately. I am very sure that a great many large companies in that area have sought employees with the highly specific skills from the schools, and have worked with the schools for the development of such skills.

The general point is that these men, who are personally typical of those in personnel work in American industry, are not seeking the sort of narrow training that would develop docile robots. The individual meeting these criteria should be a reasonably effective member of a family group and of a democratic community. But the specifications quite obviously fall short of demanding training for some of the broader aspects of citizenship or for the appreciation of literature and art, the development of tastes and interests which make for a rich personal life. Yet although these men did not list good citizenship as a prerequisite in the young men and women they wished to employ, I am certain they would be quick to feel that the omission of training for that purpose would be a mistake.

They have come to feel that collective bargaining and labor organization have a real and permanent place in industry and are anxious to have employees who are ready to take a constructive part in that activity.

I think they would favor a review of the development of our traditions, of our business, and of our political institutions as a background for that sort of contribution, as well as the necessity for intelligent citizenship, if we are going to preserve political democracy and free enterprise as an economic system.

It is obvious that they would hope that any such review would include the achievements as well as the shortcomings of American industry, and the conclusion that on the whole the political and economic system has made for reasonable well-being and happiness of the citizens.

Beyond that they would not deny the value of any training which would help the aesthetic and intellectual development of these young people to the highest degree possible.

My general feeling has been that the conflict between vocational and general education has been made much sharper than there is any reason to have it. The things which these personnel people desire in their younger employees is, after all, the sort of thing that more general education will contribute greatly to. The final aim might well be an all-around individual who enjoys life, who is a good comrade, who sees the problems and accepts the responsibility of citizenship, who has knowledge of the skill needed to earn his living at the level of his capacity. Such an individual can make the greatest contribution to his family, the community, and employers alike.

DR. WOLFSON: I do not see how one can plan a program of effective vocational education in a highly industrialized society such as ours without having an estimate of what our social needs are—and that estimate being done in advance. It is essential that we have an estimate of what our available skills are, as well as an estimate of what commodities our industries are going to produce and what kind of skills we need not only for the immediate future but also for the long-term point of view. Otherwise, training, of today, will be obsolete tomorrow. Workers who spend time, energy, and money in acquiring a vocation will find it a complete loss before they have reaped any return on their investment. I think that the so-called free enterprise economy has woefully failed in meeting this particular need.

Whatever vocational education we have had in the past and whatever we are likely to have in the immediate future must, I think, bear in mind the fact that we failed to plan in this field as well as in many others. We have learned a lesson, it seems to me, during this present war economy. Skills had to be acquired within a short time. Machines had to be changed to adapt to new workers. The War Manpower Commission was created to fulfill a certain need for planning; to shift workers where they were needed, to retrain them when necessary. In the past we failed to do that.

I should like to point out, furthermore, that vocational education in the past has closely followed the patterns of our social clichés. I am speaking now pretty much from my own experience as a teacher. If a boy or a girl is poor in his studies in high school or college, he or she is sent to a vocational school to learn a trade—the idea being that that is the only thing he or she is good for! The very fact that we have had the social pattern of thinking that learning a trade is something that morons or intellectual misfits can achieve, gives us some idea of the way in which we hold the whole matter of acquiring a skill. To work with one's hands is declassé. I think that that particular concept for a highly industrialized society such as ours, has been bad in the past, and it certainly is likely to be very bad in the immediate future.

Mr. Bridgman pointed out the fact that our vocational curriculum should include liberal subjects and thought-provoking material—and I agree with him there. But I should like to point out also that in the vocational schools that I have had anything to do with, teachers were men and women who for the most part had worked in industry, who had, perhaps, retired from industry, took three credits in New York University or at Teachers College and acquired the elements of pedagogy, and who then became teachers in our vocational schools. Their knowledge of economic and social problems or of the economic and social world in which they lived was certainly inadequate for the so-called liberalizing function that we all agree is essential.

Let me also point out that a great many of the vocational schools in the past have been known by trade unions as being centers for the preparation of "scabs." I don't think that that is as true at the present time when the trade union strength has increased so immeasurably. But, certainly, those who have followed the history of the Manhattan Trade School and some of the other trade schools in New York City know that for many years—and this is, undoubtedly, in part labor's fault as well as the fault of the pedagogues at the schools—these schools turned out men and women for specific occupations in industries, in the millinery industry, needle trades, or whatever industries they were training these workers for, with no concept of trade union principles or the principles of collective bargaining, with no concept of what the industry was about, or what the workers as an important part of the industry had in the way of responsibilities. Most of the old-time unionists have had a feeling that some of these vocational schools are something you keep away from, because they are hot-beds of anti-unionism.

I should like, also, to present the attitudes of some of our so-called middle-class families who are often cursed with youngsters who have manual dexterity, who love working with their hands, who love working with tools, who hate studies. No respectable middle-class family want to send their child to a school where he might learn a trade, because "that just isn't done!" Consequently, we have a situation, and we have had this situation up until the war, where people who might be extremely effective workers in an essential area because of manual dexterity and skills were kept from those areas by virtue of social clichés and social tradition. I am sure that all of us know of examples in our families, of individuals who were never permitted to work with their hands because it was looked down upon by the social community.

A great many of these attitudes have changed, both in World War I and World War II, and that is understandable. A war does precipitate a labor shortage. And a labor shortage means that you have got to get skilled workers or as many skilled workers as you can within a comparatively short period of time. What Mr. Bridgman pointed out as to the current necessity for speeding up skills, for breaking down skills, for developing new techniques, certainly took place in World War I as well.

The public vocational schools were very slow to meet these needs, and Mr. Bridgman's point is well taken, that industry itself had to start training-within-industry programs or vestibule schools or upgrading techniques within the plant, in order to create the necessary labor supply for the occupations that they had available.

Why did these schools lag behind? Partly because equipment and teaching were antique. Retired machinists who worked as teachers were not aware of the dynamic changes which were taking place in industry. Pressures became great and the need for new workers with new skills forced the public vocational schools and industry to combine. I understand Curtiss-Wright and some of the other war plants have worked out programs of cooperation with local vocational schools.

The experience of World War I resulted in an increase in what we call semi-skilled workers, and I am inclined to believe that the Second World War will also result in an increase in such workers, that is workers who have achieved within two or three weeks a specific skill for a specific industry, without having any knowledge of the industry or the occupation or the general industrial world. If we do have a post-war depression we will be confronted with the same kind of problems that we were confronted with after World War I; that is, an increase in the number of semi-skilled workers and large numbers of them on the breadlines or unemployment lines, or what have you. The so-called unskilled worker may be able to find a job more easily because he has acquired no special skill and has, therefore, a greater adaptability as well as a lower wage rate. The depression following the last war, particularly the 1929 depression, found industry retooling and acquiring new machinery, but those workers who were thrown out of work were frozen with their old skills and their semi-skills, and were certainly unable to adjust. . . .

The bill now in Congress which is popularly known as the GI Bill of Rights makes certain provisions that are generally understood by a great many people and exaggerated by a great many others. It is estimated, however, that it will not take care of more than one million returning soldiers and sailors. It offers a year of education—either in school or college, or some vocational training; it offers approximately two years of education for 165,000 soldiers. There is nothing in that (and I recognize its generosity, its importance and significance in our postwar program), however, that will assume responsibility for the demobilized civilian, the civilian who is demobilized from war industries. We have in that field a great deal of talk, but no plans and no specific understanding of what we are going to do with the skills that workers have acquired in the war industries, or the way in which we are going to handle them in the postwar period.

Like Dr. Burtt I feel that we have got to challenge our own social concepts with reference to the position of a manual skill in our society. I think that our academic institutions ought to have more and more of a vocational slant; that they ought to recognize the merits and the validity of a job and of work as a part of the *whole* man. On the other hand, I decry the techniques that have been used in the vocational training schools in the past, because I think that they have assumed that the person who was training in the schools, was a robot who had no concept of social thinking, who had no interest in his social responsibility, who had no interest in his role as a trade union member or as a member of a larger community group, and that all he was being prepared for was the acquisition of a skill. That is not only true of the worker in the airplane plant but also true of the professors, the physician, the chemist, the scientist whose background has been primarily technical and not at all social.

DR. LERNER: I would say that vocational education is a misnomer. There is vocational training, but education is never vocational. Everybody needs a general education as well as specific training for his job. If we think of it in this way we may get to see the issue more clearly and we shall not be so hurt by the thought that a certain amount of training is quite devoid of social significance, and be more prepared to accept the fact that much of our training is purely technical and can be acquired quite satisfactorily from teachers who are completely ignorant of our social problems or even have most pernicious ideas about them. Our discomfort may be lessened when we note, as Mr. Bridgman has pointed out, that a good deal of technical training is not of an extremely specialized kind but of a more generalized nature in which students acquire not particular skills but an ability to adapt themselves and to acquire more particular skills as they find they need them in their work. Such more generalized training is more like education than like training.

But with the advantages of teaching general adaptability rather than very specialized skills comes a great danger that is close to the heart of our problem. What happens then is that young men and women who have had this more general training come into a firm and get their particular training in the firm or in schools belonging to the plant itself. There then arises in acute form the danger that their general education, which might have gone on side by side with their special training in the general school, will suddenly come to a stop.

Even more serious is the danger of the specialized training being accompanied by education that does harm rather than good—an indoctrination of students with a particular point of view—often quite subconscious. This latter danger is by no means absent even when the training is acquired in the general school. Any teacher has to be concerned with his trainees being able to find jobs, and it is naturally easier to find jobs if his way of looking at things is close to and sympathetic with that of the people who are going to give the jobs, but the danger is greater the closer the teacher and the students are to their prospective employers.

If we do not confuse training with education we will be less likely to feel that we must rely on coincidence of good trainers also being good educators. We will be able to recognize the natural tendency for a man who is giving the training to have a point of view peculiar to people steeped in their peculiar training and absorbed in their particular business. Therefore I think we should in general expect the education we want to be provided separately.

As Professor Burtt has pointed out there is the danger that the student seeking training will want to skip the education, and this is especially true if the relevance of the general education is not seen by the student. Here we come across the general dilemma of all education—that the person who is going to be educated has to want what he is given and often he does not want it until he has already been educated to know why it is good. We have a vicious circle.

Perhaps just a little authoritarianism might be in order in applying some pressure to students to take the things which they will learn to understand and appreciate only when they already have them. But more effective than any authoritarianism (which might have the opposite effect to that intended) would be to make great efforts to show definitely and emphatically the relation of the education to the particular training.

One element in such a plan would be to have in every training school courses devoted to debunking the peculiar habits of thought of the particular professions! In the engineering school there should be a course with an anti-engineering philosophy, and similarly in other schools, and this course should concern itself with the particular foibles of engineers, etc. It should also interest itself in the basic problem of what society owes the engineer and what the engineer owes to society. I think such an approach, in definitely recognizing the biases that tend to exist rather than in hoping they will not exist, is not only more realistic but more effective. It is not a case for inculcating a definite point of view. We want rather to be sure that different points of view are put up, the different sides, and that the student acquires the art of listening to the different sides and thinking about the issues himself.

DR. WALSH: The vocational training given during the war has been short training. People by the million have learned jobs that they could learn in six weeks' time. It may be that a pretty good job has been done by finding out the aptitudes—"aptitude" is a word that goes through the vocational literature—of the people and suiting the individual to the particular job with a very short training. I suggest the necessity in vocational training of examining attitudes as distinct, from aptitudes. For example, I am confident that a lot of people have jobs today, probably millions of them, as a result of the war and the six weeks' training that they have had, who think that that is all you need to get and keep a job. They are dead wrong. We are headed straight for trouble to the degree that we have cultivated the notion that that kind of training will have competitive advantage in the job market following the war.

Confining ourselves to vocational training alone, I am concerned lest we have cultivated the notion widely that after the war there will be jobs for everybody. I know some schools which are operating on that assumption. It is a mistaken assumption. It badly prepares the individual for what is going to be his experience after the war.

Attitudes need to be examined; the attitude of the individual toward the future, the chance of jobs, the right to jobs—all that sort of thing.

Dr. Wolfson: Would you include in attitudes the question of prejudices? The question of attitudes with reference to the women workers, or the Negro workers?

Dr. Walsh: By all means. I am glad to write that in at this point because it is relevant to the observation I am attempting to make.

Vocational training as such has in most instances to be specialized. In addition to educating the boys and girls who are being trained for particular vocations there is the question of the kind of training. It is of the utmost importance that education be provided of a kind that will make the students understand the sort of world economy they are going to live in, the kind of problems they will confront as individuals. These problems need a collective attention, a group attention. Therefore, students should be prepared to exercise their responsibilities as citizens.

It is to be deplored that there are schools today that are giving good vocational training but are not lifting the blinders from the minds of their students at all regarding the whole question of what we need to do in order to achieve a fully functioning economy as we move from a war to a peace-time society.

Then there are the prejudices about free enterprise, freedom from governmental interventions—and all that kind of thing. Those are biases and prejudices that in my opinion run contrary to facts of our future needs as a nation. These are left untouched or unchallenged in many schools where vocational training is being carried on at a high level of technical competence. This is a misfortune. Then in some places there is indoctrination taking place. It may be sincere on the part of those carrying it out, but it is bad education. It is going to sow trouble for the individuals in question and for all of us.

DR. LERNER: Would you not say that that is a very good reason for being afraid of letting vocational education—I use that phrase now—be conducted by private corporations? I don't think we should prohibit it, but it is something which ought to be looked upon as a social responsibility and conducted by agencies which naturally can be expected to take a wider point of view, such as you can not expect the private corporation to do.

DR. WALSH: I agree with that. The people who go through vocational training should receive other kinds of education than that which many vocational schools give and depend upon. In order to provide that, it must be established as a principle that either the community participate in defining the curriculum or that other groups be associated with the training than simply the company or industry. I am thinking particularly of the trade unions; also—as mentioned in Professor Burtt's paper—the cooperative movement. I understand the Farmers' Union has been thinking along these lines a great deal, and has some productive suggestions. The unions themselves are deficient in this matter. They have historically confined themselves to vocational training in a narrow sense. But I find a growing realization in their ranks of the importance of the broader question.

In the Auto Workers Union, for example, efforts are being made to produce a curriculum that will be of educational signicance beyond mere vocational training. It is under joint control, the supervision of the union and the company. Where they set up vocational classes, they supplement them with classes in economics, politics, or sociology. They use teachers from colleges and high schools of the communities where the classes are conducted. The curriculum is worked out jointly by the representatives of the personnel offices of the companies and the education offices of the union. Teachers who are available and who are interested enough to give their time or to work at night with classes are used. A self-selection goes on which probably yields teachers that are fairly well suited to carry on the study they are in charge of. I think the teachers are good. Nothing more than that is feasible now.

DR. WOLFSON: I should like to point out a problem that we have on our campus, which I am sure must be duplicated all over the country, with reference to a type of vocational training and a kind of vocational isolationism, if you please. I discussed with a colleague of mine the question of the discovery of a quinine substitute at Harvard by two brilliant young chemists. I said that I thought it was too bad that Harvard, which had fathered these two boys, as it were, had turned over the results to a private company, which I understand is under some form of indictment by the Anti-Trust Division of the Department of Justice. He said: "Well, that is not our responsibility. We are, essentially, chemists. We have no responsibility for the social world or what happens to our discoveries. We are not concerned with that. Our big job is to find these things; that is what we are trained for. You are foolish to expect us to do anything more than that."

DR. WALSH: I think we have all confronted that. Scientists are among the most ignorant people in the world. They frequently are proud of their ignorance on social and economic questions. That is an indictment of the education they have received. Since science has drawn to it some of the best minds of our time, and has done so for a number of generations, it is a matter of more than ordinary importance.

It seems to me a simple proposition. Everybody who has the ability to learn at all about the economic and political problems of society should do so, even if he happens to be a scientist.

8

THE TEACHING OF DOGMATIC RELIGION IN A DEMOCRATIC SOCIETY

A. Eustace Haydon, *Professor of Comparative Religion, University of Chicago, Chairman.*
Sophia L. Fahs, *Union Theological Seminary.*
Horace L. Friess, *Professor of Philosophy, Columbia University.*
Alain Locke, *Professor of Philosophy, Howard University.*
Conrad H. Moehlman, *Professor of the History of Christianity, Colgate-Rochester Divinity School.*
Charles W. Morris, *Professor of Philosophy, University of Chicago.*

THE ARGUMENT
Horace L. Friess

CAN WE LOCATE the difficulties that dogmatism presents in relation to democracy and religion? A democratic society has need of special faith in the value of shared experience and deliberation in reaching decisions. Whatever undermines this special faith is a threat to such a society. Dogmatic religion contains this kind of threat when individuals or groups, first, claim a certainty of revelation that makes human criticism irrelevant and impertinent; and again, second, when they claim to be the preeminent bearers of a supreme value, and so justified in bidding for a controlling or even exclusive authority. I submit that dogmatism in these two senses is not only harmful to democratic society, but is also a mistaken service to religion and to God, because of the restrictions it presumes to place upon religious creation and even upon the divine greatness.

In a political sense freedom *of* religion means that neither state nor church shall compel people to adhere to a system of religion which they do not voluntarily accept, and shall allow them, without civil or political discrimination, opportunity to worship according to such systems as they do so accept. The classic defense of this principle is splendid as far as it goes, but leaves important questions unconsidered. And the failure to consider them has made possible a serious confusion in our day between "freedom *of* religion" and a vague, unexamined assumption of "freedom *for* religion."[1] The situation to which I refer can be briefly explored by taking Jefferson's classic defense of religious freedom as a starting-point. In his *Notes on Virginia* (1782) Jefferson wrote: "It does me no injury for my neighbor to say there are twenty gods, or no God. It neither picks my pocket nor breaks my leg." His argument was that religion should not be coerced, and that "reason and free inquiry are the only effectual agents against error." For its defense of individual belief and its appeal to reason and free inquiry Jefferson's statement holds our assent, yet it seems to overlook something important, namely the largely *social* character of religious beliefs. When beliefs held by millions of people as members of organizations qualifies those organizations, for instance, for tax exemption and military service exemptions, then the question can at least be sensibly raised whether some other people's pockets are not being picked and even legs broken. It is significant that what we have been asked to discuss in this Conference is not "Individual belief in dogmatic religion" but rather "The teaching of dogmatic religion." This emphasis on the *teaching of* shows that the character of a social process is at stake.

My esteemed colleague, Professor W. P. Montague, argues that personal religion is very precious, but that organized religion is almost bound to be mainly bad.[2] His estimate of the latter may well be faulty, and in any case for better or worse organized religion is likely to persist as part of society. Is it not clear, however, that society can not afford to allow as broad and unqualified a freedom to the organized *teaching of religion* as it can to individual belief? This indeed seems obvious, but it is far from obvious *what conditions of freedom to teach* democratic societies can wisely grant to groups rejecting the relevance of human criticism to any of their dogmas and pushing claims to preeminent or exclusive religious authority. The question thus raised has its application to any case of large-scale control throughout the spheres of education, scientific research, and technical invention, but presents some peculiarly stubborn difficulties in the field of religion. How far are we to encourage the view that freedom of religion

1. For this and other important distinctions see the review article by Joseph L. Blau in *The Review of Religion*, November 1944, entitled "The Freeborn Mind."
2. See his article entitled "Religion After the War" in the volume edited by Ruth Wanda Anshen, *Beyond Victory*, Harcourt Brace, New York, 1943.

involves freedom from criticism on the ground that religion is God's work and not man's? How far are we to indulge in the paradox now so widely cultivated that the welfare of a democracy depends ultimately on the spread of forms of religious faith, dogma, and teaching that are far from democratic?

These problems are especially difficult because it is so hard to be sure just what functions religious systems actually do perform. Democracies, like other societies, accord privilege and support to religion on the assumption that it serves life in valuable and even indispensable ways. But it is a path of dangerous irresponsibility to allow forms of authority to develop without reference to competence. Do religious bodies know how to shape the goals and methods of modern men? Do they actually aim to shape them in a democratic sense? Neither question can be answered with an entire affirmative. When the Rev. Dr. Buttrick looks favorably on "daily religious worship and instruction in secular schools" (*New York Times,* May 12, 1944), how well has he considered his ends and the effectiveness of the means to further them? Studies thus far made do not suggest that formal religious instruction in schools or Sunday schools bears much relation to establishing life-values, or even to securing attachment to the church. Family life seems to have much more influence on both.[3]

Nevertheless, it certainly is vital for democratic societies to give religion its due scope. For the fellowship, the perspectives, and the grace which religious bodies afford within the pattern of life do serve men indispensably. To many they furnish elements of security and of consecration which make it possible for life to continue and be renewed. They help many to make their peace with the universe on worthy terms. They provide channels for the expression and crystallization of attitudes and views which in part help to build common faith and purpose. They organize important social works. They inspire and quicken many with their ideals of personality and of God. In the fulfillment of such religious functions dogmatism, in at least one sense of the word, is probably a necessary factor. That is to say, it is doubtful whether these things could be done without involving that aspect of dogmatism which consists in affirming undemonstrated and even indemonstrable propositions.[4] To try to remove dogmatism in this sense from

3. In estimating the effects of religious instruction and proposals to extend public support of it in relation to the schools, careful attention should be given to a recent book by another participant in this panel discussion, namely C. H. Moehlman, *School and Church: The American Way,* New York, Harper & Brothers, 1944.
4. Professor Charles Morris and others participating in the discussion objected that too much may be conceded here. If the affirming of undemonstrated propositions is coupled with a willingness to submit them to continued testing, they say it can not properly be termed "dogmatic." I hope that, however the term "dogmatic" may be circumscribed, I have made sufficiently clear throughout my basic agreement that continued testing of beliefs is a need both of democracy and of religion.

religion seems to me an extreme scientific puritanism with which I am not in sympathy. Scientific inquiry should be brought to bear in all possible ways upon questions of the meaning and validity of religious doctrines, but without limiting teachability in the religious field to such doctrines as can pass strictly scientific tests. For such limitation, assuming that it could even be instituted, would work to eliminate not only much rubbish but also idea-forces of great and perhaps essential value to human development.

IN THE PRESENT GENERATION a new thing has happened. The main traditions of European culture have been put in such jeopardy that America is now viewed not only as a refuge for dissenting minorities but as a vital ground on which to help save the major orthodoxies. This is the immediate significance of current neo-Thomism and of the neo-Reformation theologies in our midst today. And it will reward us to consider the various bearings of these movements as understandingly and realistically as we can. The official endorsement of Thomism by Rome must be seen as part of a long process of making the Roman Church administration more constitutional. Neo-Reformation theology has sought to revive a central historic core of Protestant faith and to use it to criticize the complacencies and check the disintegrating tendencies in modern culture. These motives should have some appeal to lovers of democracy whatever they may think of the means employed to realize them. At the same time whoever will look freely at the whole world-wide scene spread out before us today must also feel, I think, that both neo-Thomism and neo-Reformation theology are now helplessly parochial. And most Americans must feel too that these movements are associated with traditions that have accorded churches a different political and cultural status than we have been accustomed to accord them in this country. Parochial ways of thought seeking preferential status must suffer suspicion in a democracy even though they espouse some important democratic values.

Ardent proponents of any faith are apt to claim as great a rôle as possible for their cause. It should not be astonishing to hear that the world can be saved only by Catholicism, or by Protestant realism, for we hear the same kind of claim sometimes made for Ethical Culture, for democracy, and for the scientific spirit. To think that the world can be saved in some one way alone seems to me, however, either a naïve faith, or else a symptom of an anxiety neurosis, or perhaps there is a third alternative: it may be just propaganda. Such a statement, of course, does not imply a condemnation of these various movements themselves, for each of them may well save something less, or perhaps more, than the world, in other words may save some souls. And along with its saving powers, whatever these be, each movement may have further cultural functions of moment. Thus neo-Thomism and the neo-Reformation theologies are both posing anew some very important questions for contemporary culture. What is to be the place of metaphysics in the intellectual organization of culture? What is the rôle of myth or its equivalents? And what place is Hebrew-Christian tradition to have in the future building of spiritual community?

These are questions which many liberals apparently thought sufficiently settled so that they could forget about them. It is my impression that they were thus caught napping in their own dogmatic slumbers, and perhaps have not yet awakened to a very serious consideration of these and other questions posed by the neo-orthodox movements. Furthermore, many liberals in their commitment to democratic faith apparently forgot that there are basic material and spiritual needs whose partial satisfaction at least must be presupposed if distinctively democratic values are to have much of a chance. People too insecure physically and spiritually do not make good democrats. In this sense it is true that democracy requires some foundations that are not necessarily of its own making. But this is far from implying that those fundamental material and spiritual securities cannot, in the nature of things, be achieved in democratic ways, and that they can only be achieved in authoritarian ways unfavorable to democracy.

What it does imply is that society requires these fundamental needs to be met, if not in democratic then in other ways. And from this one may conclude that liberalism needs to expand its interests and methods once again rather than to follow a defensive course of contracting them. Instead of clutching only one arrow in its quiver—the scientific spirit—even though it be an especially true and reliable one, it is necessary to be bold again as in earlier days to declare visions and larger perspectives more imaginatively than liberals have done for a long time. In a day when immediate circumstances are bound to be full of frustration for millions of people, indeed for us all, we can ill afford to resign all the appeal of the transcendent and of far-off goals into the hands of authoritarian groups. It will also be unfortunate if ritual and devotional resources come entirely into such hands. Nor should authoritarian groups be able to pose as the appointed guardians of the wisdom of the ages, in view of all that the liberal spirit has accomplished in the last century to add to our knowledge and understanding of the past. But more than all, instead of merely parrying misinformed attacks on project methods and activity programs in education, liberals are basically challenged in the present time to work out many far greater projects linking education and social construction dynamically in small relations, on TVA scale, and on still larger scale. Indeed it is very largely because the programs of the authoritarian groups offer an obstruction to such efforts that there is occasion to be troubled by them.

With respect to religion what prospect, I wonder, does each of us cherish for its future? Answering for myself I confess hope that, with the development of society, man's consecrations and ways of making his peace with the universe will eventually be worthy again of the great past of religion. With the fuller meeting of eastern and western peoples it seems to me likely that certain personal values and attitudes hitherto most explicitly cultivated in Hebrew-Christian traditions will become more widely spread, but also that other values in the past more cultivated in the religious traditions of India and of China—values of detachment and of objective social relations—will also be spread. Here I find myself in much agreement with views expressed by Professor Morris in his book *Paths of Life*.[5] But I would not know by what old and new names these more widely diffused values and attitudes are most likely to become recognized. I also confess to not being concerned in the first instance about the names, and certainly not, as many seem to be, that all good things be called by one sacred name.

No doubt there are many who think it is just this pluralism in liberalism—which they interpret as indifferentism—that has been responsible for the weakening of religion and perhaps for the crisis in modern culture. Plausible though it may seem on the surface there is reason to think that this explanation is only superficial. The crisis came also to countries like Italy, Spain, and Japan with relatively homogeneous religious patterns. Moreover, in times past many societies and cultures have succeeded in giving significant place to vigorous and diverse religious faiths. The attempt seems worth continuing in the interest both of democratic society and of spiritual development. As far as the weakening of religion in modern times is concerned, impressive evidence could be gathered for attributing it, not to the decline of dogmatic religious monopolies, but rather to the failure of dogmatic churches to realize and correct the inadequacies of their own traditions.

Professor Jacques Maritain, in recent writings for "Reconciliation of the Gospel and Democracy," has put forward two propositions in these words:

First, I think that the world has done with what is called neutrality. Willingly or unwillingly, States will be obliged to make a choice for or against the gospel. They will be shaped either by the totalitarian or by the Christian spirit.

Second, at the same time the State should be fully aware of its merely

5. *Ibid.*

secular standing and realize that it has no power on sacred matters nor on men's consciences.[6]

Taking these statements just in themselves there seems to be a large ambiguity in them; but taking them in the context of affairs today I wish I could think they were more ambiguous. I wish I could think that Professor Maritain meant only that states must become more forbearing and essentionally Christian in their politics, and at the same time refrain from exercising compulsion in matters of worship and the like. For to such an interpretation.I might eagerly say "Amen, and pray show us the way." But it is all too evident that there is a far different meaning, namely renewed reliance of the state for the moral and spiritual education of its citizens upon the controlling sacred sources of Judaeo-Christian traditions. Perhaps Professor Maritain from his point of view would even find it difficult to distinguish these two possible interpretations of his statements.

But it seems important to point out that though the separation of church and state has its good and more than sufficient reasons, it is often advocated for reasons that can be harmful in their consequences for both religion and democratic society. To suppose, for instance, that church and state must be separated in order to divorce religion and politics is to entertain an illusion that this can really be done. Furthermore, one motive underlying the attempted divorce has been to defend an absolute authority for the church at least in some sphere of "faith and morals" and for the state in the sphere of legal adjustment. This should be considered a bad motive by all who are opposed to institutional absolutism in either sphere. Personally I should not want to grant absolute authority over faith and morals to any institution, nor to depart from that federalism in government which involves the denial of absolute legal authority to any single system of laws. Absolutism departmentalized tends towards something lifeless and mechanical in both the secular and the religious sphere.

The good reason for a separation of church and state is not to divorce religion and politics, but to prevent either church or state from obtaining an actual monopoly in either sphere. It is an interest in freedom. To the extent that church and state are persuaded to relinquish their absolutistic, not to say totalitarian, tendencies, there is much less need of their separation. The remark has its bearing on the politics of "Establishment" in England, for example. But seeing that church and state are not so thoroughly persuaded to relinquish absolutistic claims, and perhaps never can be, what recourses has a democratic society in the interest of freedom? It has two. The first consists in checking one absolutism by the other, hence their

6. *Current Religious Thought.* IV, 4, April 1944. Cf. the further development of these points in Maritain's recent book, *Christianity and Democracy*, New York, Scribners, 1944.

separation. A second consists in seeing to it that many religious and many legal functions are actually performed by groups and organizations that are not making absolutistic claims. Continued vigorous and flourishing development along this second line is of great importance, I think, to democratic society.

The relation between religion and a democratic society is not in either direction like that between a master and a servant. Ideally the relation of such a society to religion is more like that between artists and the arts; actually it is more like that obtaining between people generally and the arts. My argument throughout this discussion is not based on claiming complete and exclusive value for democracy, putting it somehow in the place of God and asking religion only to serve democracy. On the other hand, I cannot agree with Professor Maritain that democratic states have "merely secular standing" with "no power on sacred matters nor on men's consciences." I cannot agree that the distinctive values of democratic faith are merely secular, and certainly not that they are merely secular applications of traditional Hebrew-Christian religious values. There are new elements of religious meaning in the democratic methods of shared experience and deliberation, and also in the democratic objective of the maximum possible development of all.

What has happened historically may be briefly described as follows: When people found that they could not rely on the churches to forward these distinctively democratic values adequately, many undertook to cultivate independent sources and expressions of democratic faith. Such faith has been cultivated in theistic and deistic, in transcendental, in ethical and in humanistic terms as well as in terms of the older religious traditions. Today the neo-orthodox are directing their counter-attacks against the newer accents of faith. The more democratically-minded among them are trying to convince men that democracy can be safe and prosper only under the blessing of the traditional Hebrew-Christian faith. The newer terms of democratic faith are criticized as "utopian" and guilty of human pride, the sin with a capital S, or as having "a political-minded conception of religion" which leads inevitably to secular totalitarianism in some nationalistic, communistic, or other form. Many important things are to be learned from these criticisms for all faiths, but I should not list among them the wisdom of reliance in democracy on one single saving faith—not even in "the scientific spirit and democratic faith."

The issue I am raising here is not the special issue of humanism, but of creation and of restriction in the whole sphere of religion. The problems involved are those of the functions and methods of religion and of a suitable distribution of authority for their advancement in a democratic society. I maintain that it is a religious, and not merely a secular, function of a democratic state to seek to provide conditions for the freest and fullest development of its members in the religious as in the other dimensions of life. With this in mind I should like to close my remarks with a word of prayer and of confession. To the spirit of deliverance I pray: May we be delivered from the dogmatic teaching that the world can be saved by Christianity alone, or ethics alone, or democracy alone, or the scientific spirit alone! And to the spirit of creation I pray: May we become more ethical, and more democratic, and more scientific, and more full of Christ and the prophets and sages of all the world! My confession is this: I believe that these two spirits of deliverance and of creation here invoked in truth and in life are one spirit.

THE DISCUSSION

DR. MORRIS: That a democratic society cannot but oppose dogmatism (in the sense of claims of a certainty of revelation that makes human criticism irrelevant and impertinent; and claims for a preeminent and perhaps monopolistic authority), and that a democratic society cannot commit itself to any dogmatic religion, nor remain unconcerned about religions which undermine democratic attitudes, is I think clear and very important. I also agree that the historic religions have failed us in certain respects rather than that our difficulties come from our failure to accept them; and that there is a new religious core in the democratic attitude itself. Any attitude which exercises a dominant control over our life is religious in tone, and the democratic attitude is often of this sort. My comments center around Professor Friess's acceptance of the need for dogmatism in the sense of "affirming undemonstrated and even undemonstrable propositions."

Such dogmatism, he writes, "is probably a necessary factor in building religious confidence in valuable ways." Whether this is so or not depends on what is meant by the "affirmation of an undemonstrated proposition." There is a sense in which such affirmation is an inherent part of all thought and action. A mathematician may believe that a proposition which is not demonstrated is in fact demonstrable, and this belief may induce him to engage in long and arduous attempts at its proof; a chemist may affirm that some general principle of structural organization holds in fields where it has not been tested; a psychiatrist may prescribe a course of life to overcome a patient's difficulty, and he and the patient may work hard to give the prescription a chance. In all such cases affirmation of an unproved proposition is a necessary factor in carrying out a certain course of investigation and action. But in none of these cases is the belief dogmatic in the sense that it is not subject to modification, or even rejection, in the further development of the life process which at a given moment needs belief in the proposition. Hence we must distinguish between the dogmatic and the non-dogmatic affirmation of undemonstrated or undemonstrable propositions. And I shall argue that dogmatism in this sense is as harmful to a democratic society as the other two forms of dogmatism. Indeed, if this form is defended on the ground that it is a necessary factor in building religious confidence I am sure that voices will defend the other two forms on the same ground.

Accordingly, I contend that a dogmatic religion and the dogmatic teaching of a dogmatic religion are in the last analysis harmful to the particular temper which the term democratic suggests. For if in Friess's words faith in democracy is related to "faith in shared experience and deliberation as methods, and with the maximum possible development of all as an ideal objective," then the dogmatic holding or teaching of religious beliefs is dangerous to this faith—for it reduces respect for the experience of others and for the control of belief by deliberation, and it dulls the awareness that the development of another person may perhaps best proceed along different lines than one's own development. The democratic attitude involves flexibility, experimentation, correction of beliefs in action, respect for individuality, ability to live with diversity; and dogmatism in any form is an enemy to this attitude and a friend to its rival, the authoritarian attitude. Some people undoubtedly do need the dogmatic assertion of beliefs to give them confidence, but in so far as this is so it means we have failed to develop in them the democratic attitude. Hence I am unable to accord dogmatism even the small niche which Professor Friess has left for it, or which at least some of his readers will think he has left for it.

What of the democratic attitude itself? I see no need of a qualification here either. It is possible to act vigorously on this attitude without being dogmatic in the sense defined. At the heart of every religion there is some basic attitude which is given preeminence in the direction of life, some commitment to being one kind of a person rather than another. The democratic attitude seems to be such an attitude and commitment, and to have at least the potentialities of religious significance. In so far as it is supported by existing religions it can welcome that support. In so far as it is not it will oppose them. In so far as it is a novel attitude it will have to find novel forms of expression not furnished by any of the traditional religions. And it will not wisely commit its cause to any one of them, or to all of them together. This does not require that the democratic attitude must itself be held or taught dogmatically. It is an attitude which has been developed under given historical conditions and it can defend itself, and test itself by reference to the realities of this period of culture. The only religion appropriate to the democratic faith is a non-dogmatic religion. Or if by definition all religions are made dogmatic, then no religion is appropriate to the democratic faith.

Dogmatic religions do however exist. If they are not to be taught dogmatically, should they be taught at all, and if so how? That they should be taught stems from the fact that religious literature exemplifies the basic attitudes which men have taken to give integration and direction to their lives. And men today, with the same general problem, are entitled to have as material for their own lives whatever help they can find in the way other persons have lived. Religious literature—like that of the arts, morality, and politics—contains a rich heritage to be understood, appraised, used, or rejected. This heritage is part and parcel of human achievement, and rightly used it will not be replaced by, nor need be humble before, science. The adequate use of this heritage is the main problem for the opponents of authoritarianism. It is especially important today that such material be drawn from many cultures, so that the student will understand, and in some sense build into himself, the characteristic features of the other great cultures with which we must effectively cooperate if we are to move in the direction of a world democracy. Here too we see the importance of a non-dogmatic teaching of such material, for if we believe we must commit everyone in all cultures to one religion before cooperation is possible, we are hindering the democratic process we profess to support. Used non-dogmatically, the religious heritage can be made to contribute to the growth of the democratic individual and to the growth of a democratic world culture—and perhaps even to the growth of new religions. The authoritarian and dogmatic attitude in education—religious or otherwise—is often a sincere attempt to give education integration and focus. However, the dogmatic affirmation of beliefs leads inevitably to impatience with those who criticize these dogmas, and finally to attempts to exercise monopolistic power and authority.

The dogmatic attitude is democratically sterile since it subordinates growth to attainment, open-minded flexibility to fearsome defensiveness, creativity to security. The dogmatic attitude is the major enemy which the democratic attitude faces today on the domestic and international frontiers. It must be resisted in every one of its manifestations. It would be fatal to allow it to capture the educational process in the schools or in the churches. The best way to avoid this result is by positive action in developing educational institutions and curriculums which make as adequate a use of what has been called our normative heritage as we have made of scientific methods and results. Criticism of the dogmatists is not enough, and a stress on science—though of basic importance—is not enough. Liberals, humanists, democrats need to pass from the defensive to the offensive if they are to remain significant guardians of the contemporary outreachings of human creativity.

DR. LOCKE: It seems to me that in spite of the recent clamor to admit the teaching of religious values to the schools, especially the public schools, we must still devise some way of holding the line for our traditional school neutrality in matters of religion. For this is at least a negative democratic attitude that we have maintained. Yet, at the same time we must meet the challenge of this recent criticism that by and large we just solve by evasion the problems of moral education.

The present problem is the question of how to educate more positively in terms of the moral and even some of the cultural humanistic values of our moral inheritance. As Professor Morris says, to start out with, we ought to realize that we have not been as undogmatic as we think we have been, because even from our Colonial beginnings, it was the question of saying, Well, this freedom, this traditional freedom of ours consists in our right to be dogmatic each in his own way. In the Bay State Colony, you had your right to go out, at great hazard, to Rhode Island, to dogmatize there. Even though the situation today is apparently more tolerant, we still have a situation where one dogmatic tradition dogmatizes at a street corner, while another has the right to dogmatize in the middle of the block.

I am not discussing freedom of conscience and religious beliefs primarily. I am discussing education's predicament of being confined to a sterile neutrality by which education cannot say anything about certain important moral aspects of life at all, because of the preemption of the subject matter by the dogmatic religious traditions.

Now, I think the time has come, especially in this crisis, when education must do something about this stalemate, where it must find a sensible solution and a democratic solution, a scientifically objective solution, in not considering what it shall teach as a direct and inappropriate duty of teaching religion, but what it ought to teach informatively about religion and social morality.

Religion so conceived becomes an important phase of our whole humanistic tradition. Here, I think, instead of trying to make concessions to the dogmatic approach, we ought to make an independent scientific approach, borrowing our material from cultural anthropology and even from the sort of thing that Professor Morris has pioneered in—the over-all comparison of cultural values, religious and otherwise, particularly such value concepts as serve as life-guidance ideas and ideals. Here, I think, we are in safe territory—although pioneer territory—because as much as we now know about comparative religion and comparative culture, we have not yet focused much of this material from the point of view of the vital instruction and effective induction of students into the moral inheritance of our civilization.

Now the question, of course, becomes tremendously more complicated obviously by the perspective of our crisis today. It is made so not merely by the complex cultural character of our own national society, our own national population but by the fact that our education will more and more have to take into account the world situation, the world picture, and the great diversity of both religious beliefs and moral traditions in the world which we must consciously live in today.

On this point, though, I think we can welcome that complexity, that very substantial widening of the cultural horizons, because from the point of view of the dangers of dogmatism there is safety in greater diversity. The more of these traditions we have to review and take into account, the more intellectually ridiculous and unwarrantable the sectarian dogmatisms will appear to be. I think our proper way of countering religious sectarian dogmatism, even this new move to reintroduce formal teaching of religion into education, will be to provide this scientific, and, I think, really democratic antidote to dogmatism—the worst aspects of it—by putting first into general education a pretty thorough, critical, and objective review of the various religious traditions, their place and influence on history, and then trying to get from it with our anthropological insights, some indication of how these various traditions have served large groups of people for the guidance of life.

I should like to add a short postscript along this line; that the tradition of freedom of conscience and freedom of worship with us, stemming largely from a Protestant tradition, has emphasized the promotion of goodness in society in terms of individual initiative, individual responsibility, and the control of conscience. We know that that has not been any too effective in bringing about the good society. In fact, it seems to me that one of the penetrating analyses of the situation is Professor Niebuhr's—that such individualization of morals has practically resulted in what he has called the paradoxical situation of moral man in a fundamentally immoral society.

The democratic emphasis in the matter of religion ought not to be upon beliefs and dogma, but upon what effects in human relationships the beliefs and dogma have. The democratic approach, therefore, to this field, I think, could in a way reveal common denominators among all the creeds and all of the religions. It could very well focus on the necessity of promoting the good society, and what is necessary to promote a good society. Here we have a situation that can be objectively approached if we look at sin in the social aspect and try to focus on what religion and morality and even humanistic values normally can do to alleviate poverty and want and suffering, economic exploitation and so on.

So, with the emphasis on the social rôle of moral values and moral ideals in their specific promotion of a good and a better society, I think we have something where we can safely and constructively approach the teaching of our moral inheritance by the schools, even by the public schools, and where we can have a somewhat objective gauge of the relative effectiveness of various religious bodies and various religious traditions with respect to what they have actually done towards making society better.

MRS. FAHS: It is a dangerous thing at this time to try to inject into our public school system any kind of religious education. Even we who are called educators are not sufficiently educated in religion to know how to do it. The method that is now in vogue of releasing children to go in groups to their respective churches for instruction is entirely inadequate, because we are thereby fostering unscientific procedures in the study of religion and are giving our children over to untrained and unsupervised teachers who regard their class periods as opportunities for religious indoctrination.

That there are dogmatic and even fanatical religious groups in our society we must admit. If we persecute them or try to exclude them from participation in our democracy, we ourselves would be undemocratic. Nor can we rightfully dictate what people should think and what they should not think or believe. It is worth paying a great price to preserve our religious freedom.

On the other hand, it has been pointed out that we are unrealistic when we try to separate religion from life and from general education. Religion has always been woven into the warp and woof of life. It is in history, it is in science, it is in every form of human experience. It is not only the Alpha and Omega of life; it is the very meaning of life. Religious beliefs furnish the framework within which other thinking is contained. They also often provide the motivation for certain types of action and they remove the impetus to other patterns of behavior.

Recognizing this permeating and vital character in religion, we have as a people grown dissatisfied with the present complete elimination of religious education from general education. But if we are to move away from this traditional separation of religion, there is but one path which we can safely follow if our freedom is to be preserved. In any plan that is related to our public education, the only safe way is to relinquish for ourselves (and to see to it that others also relinquish) all direct concern with the propagating of any one kind of religious belief or pattern of ritual. The only religious education appropriate in our public schools or in any way linked to our public schools, is one which deals *with the process only* by which children and young people may achieve religious faith. It is appropriate, however, in our public schools to help children to apply to religion the processes of inquiry, of gathering of the facts of human experience, of comparing values and of choosing for themselves in the light of their understanding, what appeals to them as most nearly true and best.

It is appropriate for public school children to have an opportunity to become intelligent regarding how and why men have been religious, to become acquainted with the teachings of pioneers of different faiths whose influence has changed the life habits of millions of people. It is appropriate for public school children to have the opportunity to appreciate some of the literary, artistic, and musical heritage which religion in its varied forms has bequeathed mankind. But these processes are appropriate only if they can be followed without submitting children to pressure to follow any one line of tradition. Such a religious education would mean the applying to the religious field the same processes of scientific inquiry as the public schools seek to encourage in other areas of life.

The difficulties in setting up such religious education in our public schools are many and great. First and foremost is the fact that practically all leaders in education, whether in the religious or in the general field, have considered the teaching of religion as a means of affirming those propositions which Dr. Friess has shown are undemonstrable and as a way of persuading people to accept these propositions as if they were factual truth. Most educators have decided that the scientific spirit cannot rightfully enter the field of religion and they, therefore, believe that we must continue to give over all instruction in this area to institutions that assume an authoritarian relationship to those whom they teach.

If as a minority group we wish to see this new way of religious education in our public schools tried out it is important, it seems to me, that we do three things at the beginning:

First of all, there should be organized a group of capable pioneers who will study and work out new curricular materials appropriate for the new process. In the second place, we need to set up experimental stations in certain public schools where the new approach can be tried out and evaluated. And in the third place, we need to establish centers where teachers and supervisors may be trained in this new way.

DR. MOEHLMAN: By implication and by overt counts in their indictments, the apologists for non-public or private education allege that the curriculum of public education is ethically inferior to that of their schools.

If these charges could be sustained, the case against public education would become serious. Public educators have been remiss in not taking them seriously and demonstrating their falsity. This is the main issue and therefore deserves refutation. Public education like Protestantism has felt itself so integral a part of American life that it has not defended itself against the insinuations of its enemies. It must now defend its right to continue.

Here, for instance, as a sample, is a volume entitled *World History: A Christian Interpretation* by Albert Hyma and J. F. Stach. It is designed as a "textbook in world history in junior high and high schools." It rejects the process, or developmental view of life. It seems to blame the world situation upon "paganized teachings promulgated in our textbooks," although Christianity has been the religion of Europe for fifteen centuries and Martin Luther was a "secularist."

What is the superior teaching the authors have in mind? I am now quoting from the volume. Is it "but Ham, the wicked son of Noah, who was the ancestor of the black race, the people who did become the servants of the white race, *as God had decreed*," page 21? Is it the paragraph "What the Christians thought of slavery" on page 126, which supports that view? Is it the misrepresentation on pages 95 and 96 that we have "age of Metternich" but no "age of Christ," when we have *Anno Domini,* that is, an era of Christ? Is it the unfair statements about the Unitarians on page 281? Is it this delicious morsel from page 415?

> We still retain our faith in the capitalistic order of society. That order has been maintained in this country for more than 200 years and whatever is wrong with society today is not because of capitalistic enterprise but *because of the sinful nature of mankind.*

This book is designed for non-public school Christian instruction, and in it you have all the old enmities brought out once more. I have before me half a dozen books along the same line. Here, for instance, is Herrmann's *Faith and Morals,* page 137, where the following is quoted from J. P. Gury, "Casus Conscientiae":

> Anna, who has been unfaithful to her marriage vow, answers her husband (who suspects it, and questions her) the first time that she has not broken their marriage relationship; the second time (after being absolved from the sin) she answers: "I am not guilty of any crime of the kind." Finally, the third time, as her husband presses her, she denies the adultery altogether, and says, "I have not committed it," meaning in her own mind, "an act of adultery which I am bound to disclose."
> Has Anna in any one of these cases acted wrongly? In all three cases Anna is to be acquitted of the charge of lying. . . .

Can we really be silent when our grandest inheritance, the public school, system of this country, is attacked as teaching inferior things on an ethical level, when we come upon matters like this?

"Principal Heresies," listed in a certain non-public school textbook, are "Anabaptism, Anglicanism, Baptists"—thank God, he knows the difference between the Anabaptists and Baptists—"Calvinism, Christian Science, Lutheranism," and so on, through the whole list of Protestant groups.

In the same book one reads: "Equivocation—the use of phrases or words having more than one meaning in order to conceal information which the questioner has no right to seek. *It is permissible to equivocate in answering impertinent and unjust questions."*

Has our public school system retained the religious values basic to our democracy only modifying them to meet the new needs of the twentieth century? The best answer is Bower's *Church and State in Education,* which seems to be advertised the country over as a sort of traditional book, but when you read it, you are amazed. He proposes a functional interpretation of religion and the indirect incorporation of its values into public education. The six values listed (pages 60 to 71) are: "Religion should be objectively dealt with;" treated as literature; practised; cultivated by the use of ceremonials and celebrations; regarded as integrating principle of culture; used in personal counseling—all of which values are already present in public education. That public education has not turned its back upon reasonable religion is also demonstrated on pages 95 to 102 of *School and Church: The American Way.*

What would the ultimate consequences of public taxation for the support of non-public schools be? Let me refer you to Burke's *Defensible Spending for Public Schools.* I never expected to find tucked away in a book upon finance, so great a wealth of information upon the dangers that lurk in the latest attempts to obtain public monies for non-public schools! The advantages resulting to groups controlling publicly financed church schools would be: 1. Escape from direct democratic control over these schools; 2. Right to impose their religious tests on teachers; 3. The promotion of their doctrines under their own censorship; 4. Ownership of their schools; 5. Retention of their general voting rights and privileges in public school matters.

The decision of the United States Supreme Court in the Louisiana textbook case (281US370) and even more the arguments in the brief against it should be know by every lover of our American public schools.

The court held in substance that "appropriations by the State of money derived from taxation to the supplying of school books free for children in private as well as in public schools is not objectionable under the 14th

Amendment as taking private property for private purposes *where the books furnished for private schools are not granted to the schools themselves but only to or for the use of the children and are the same as those furnished for public schools and are not religious or sectarian in character."*

The arguments of the brief opposing the decision of the lower court in favor of free text-books for private school children include that taxes may be levied by a State only for public purposes, that the public has a common and equal right to their use and benefit, that private schools do not come under the category of public use. Public use is the right secured to the public to enjoy the objects for which the tax is levied as well as the reservation of control. Now private schools may limit their patrons in any way they choose—race, geography, birth, sect, number, sex, etc. Moreover, the State is restricted in control of private schools as to curriculum and instructors. Free text-books for children in private schools charging tuition and requiring children to furnish text-books is AID and indirectly a state tax. The logical consequences of the grant of free text-books to private schools would therefore be that the state pay tuition, transportation salaries in part, and cost of buildings in part. The aid is not only to the individual children but a diversion of public property to private individuals without distinction as to need for charity. This division of public school funds signifies ultimately that the parents of private school pupils would not be paying their part of the public school tax. Thus the State would be prevented from taxing any who support private schools for the support of public schools.

If the arguments of this brief were to be popularized in our educational journals, the trend toward the use of public funds for private schools might be halted.

DR. HAYDON: If you look at religion in the long sweep of human history, you will find that the main emphasis is not on theological or metaphysical ideas, not on particular forms of ceremonial or ritual, not even upon some specific eternal fixed group of values. The thing that really is the central driving force running throughout all the cultures, creating all the religions of the world, is the effort of people to find the things which make life perfectly satisfying. That is, we have been trying through all these ages to learn how to live together happily, to learn how to master the material world so as to guarantee the physical basis of life upon which we could build a culture.

We find ourselves in this age of the world, with all the necessary tools, knowledge, methods, and resources available for the task. If we really were interested in building a genuine democracy, we would have religion integrated into life. All the traditional religions belong to the childhood of man. All the ancient forms were created in those groping periods when man did not have mastery, did not know enough about his world or about himself. A working democracy would be modern religion at work.

I do not want to offend the philosophers. I would hesitate to say anything mean about them, but I am convinced that the history of thought, if you follow it through the whole story of man's development, will show that most of the metaphysical systems and most of the theologies are built upon the blundering guesses of primitive man. All that the theologians have done since, and the metaphysicians after them, was to make an ever-increasing refinement of those primitive blunders.

The thing that is most important is that if we really set to work, as has been said, to integrate the values which we recognize as democratic values in life, we will have done the religious job. If we do that job, it seems to me that we do not need to worry about anything the dogmatists can say anywhere, because they will get nowhere.

To give full information, to teach the history of cultures, to show in a purely objective and scientific way the history of thought, to bring the cultures of the world into perspective so that they interpenetrate with mutual understanding is our task. That would be the end of all parochial dogmatisms. The rest of it will be simply a matter of building for our new world a philosophy of life and a program. The new philosophy will reveal to man his place in relation to the long history of his development, will give his life a mystic meaning as a growing point of the life of the planet, will place upon him full responsibility as the bearer of the cultural heritage of the ages and the creator of the new culture which will give a glorious fulfillment to the age-old religious ideals.

It is true that among the conservatives in all cultures you will find agreement, battling over ideas, worrying and questioning as to who has the right to teach what, and a constant emphasis upon traditional ideas and forms and institutions. In India and China, of course, they are not worried about ideas. They have never been intolerant in the realm of belief. There the conservatives are insisting upon ancient patterns of behavior, institutions, castes, and various forms. My confidence for the future rests upon the fact that everywhere there are men of vision who are outstanding masters of modern science, who are coming face to face with modern problems, who are working out the ideals and the programs to solve those problems—in China, in India, in Turkey, in Russia, in the Near East, in America. These religious leaders, who are following the scientific method and trying for the democratic ideal, all come together. There are no differences between Christian and Jew and Confucianist and Buddhist on that level.

THE FUTURE BELONGS TO THESE CREATIVE LEADERS, NOT TO THE DEFENDERS OF THE AUTHORITARIAN PAST.

CONTRIBUTORS TO THIS VOLUME

Comfort A. Adams, *Professor Emeritus of Electrical Engineering, Harvard University*

Floyd H. Allport, *Professor of Political and Social Psychology, Syracuse University*

Bruce Bliven, *Editor, The New Republic*

Donald Bridgman, *American Telephone & Telegraph Co.*

Edwin A. Burtt, *Professor of Philosophy, Cornell University*

A. J. Carlson, *Professor Emeritus of Physiology, University of Chicago*

Harry J. Carman, *Dean, Columbia College*

John Dewey, *Professor Emeritus of Philosophy, Columbia University*

Irwin Edman, *Professor of Philosophy, Columbia University*

Sophia L. Fahs, *Union Theological Seminary*

Horace L. Friess, *Professor of Philosophy, Columbia University*

Harry Gideonse, *President, Brooklyn College*

A. Eustace Haydon, *Professor of Comparative Religion, University of Chicago*

A. D. Henderson, *President, Antioch College*

Sidney Hook, *Chairman, Department of Philosophy, New York University*

Abba P. Lerner, *Professor of Economics, New School for Social Research*

Eduard C. Lindeman, *Professor of Social Philosophy, New York School of Social Work, Columbia University*

Alain Locke, *Professor of Philosophy, Howard University*

Lawson G. Lowrey, M.D.

Henry Margenau, *Associate Professor of Physics, Yale University*

Morris Meister, *Principal, Bronx High School of Science*

Conrad H. Moehlman, *Professor of the History of Christianity, Colgate-Rochester Divinity School*

Charles W. Morris, *Professor of Philosophy, University of Chicago*

Arthur E. Murphy, *Professor of Philosophy, University of Illinois*

Jerome Nathanson, *Leader, New York Society for Ethical Culture*

Donald A. Piatt, *Professor of Philosophy, University of California in Los Angeles*

John G. Pilley, *Chairman, Department of Education, Wellesley College*

John Herman Randall, Jr., *Professor of Philosophy, Columbia University*

Bernard B. Smith, *American Legal Consultant, British Broadcasting Corp.*

V. T. Thayer, *Educational Director, Ethical Culture Schools*

J. Raymond Walsh, *Educational Director, C.I.O.*

Gerald Wendt, *Science Editor, Time, Inc.*

Theresa Wolfson, *Professor of Economics, Brooklyn College*